The Next Arrow

Fighting Spiritual Warfare and Winning

Mo Mydlo

DEDICATION

This book is dedicated to my partner in life and the only man bold and courageous enough to handle being married this hot mess for Jesus. My Tommy has been the keeper of my heart for most of my life. His love for Jesus exudes from every fiber of his being. He is the perfect spiritual leader of our home and the most amazing husband and father anyone could ask for. He makes his job look so easy, but, I know better. He's my man and I thank God for him, daily.

Connect with Mo

For more information about Unforsaken Women Corp check out our
website, www.unforsakenwomen.com

Follow Mo on Facebook
www.facebook.com/UnforsakenMo/

Follow Mo on Twitter
https://twitter.com/momydlo

ACKNOWLEDGMENTS

I would love to recognize my sweet mama who proofread this book for me along with all of the other "free ministry duties" she performs daily to help Unforsaken Women Corporation run so efficiently. I'm more thankful than I can say in words. She gave me life, and she still is giving to all of her kids every day, every little bit of energy that she has to give.

Speaking of thankful,. I could not be more thankful than I am for my sweet daughter in the faith Angel Clark who is my right hand in ministry. She can whip through a to-do list quicker than anyone I have ever seen, all while juggling two toddlers at home. She's an amazing wife and mother and she represents the ministry well.

I could not do what I do each day without my Armor Bearers Chrissy Peterson and Kimmie Bush. Their friendships to me and service in the ministry and at home, equip me to do what I do with a smile on my face and joy in my heart. They help me to not be so serious, and they keep me from walking around with dark roots and clothes that don't match. It takes a village to keep this old country girl looking good.

I want to acknowledge the loves of my life who I petition the throne room of Heaven and claim God's promises for on a daily basis. My husband Tommy and my kids Jacob, Travis, Sara and Eli. I could never forget my daughter in law Brooke who brings such joy to our home because of her spunky personality.

At this point in my life, I am closer to being a Grandma or should I say "Mimi" than I can even hold back enthusiasm about. This book represents the good fight of faith that I have learned to fight my entire saved life to ensure a blessed future for my grandchildren and great grandchildren. It is my heart's desire to leave a lasting legacy of love for my descendants. May our quiver be filled with the pitter patter of little feet for many years to come.

A huge thank you goes out to Emily, Alfredo and Kristy Greco for the cover design. You are an amazing family of warriors for Christ.

The Next Arrow

I woke up feeling worn out. It wasn't because we were working on a project around the house, or putting on another fundraiser for our non-profit. I woke up feeling tired, from the fight. The fight that I have fought for 20 years with God. The fight that has helped me overcome the ugly demon called anxiety. The fight that the Word calls, the good fight of faith. I woke up with a spirit of defeat over me and I couldn't understand why.

Why was I so tired? I have learned how to master my poor thinking patterns through behavioral techniques, scriptural truths and prayer. I have written books about overcoming. I have helped many individuals wean themselves off of conventional anxiety medication as they learn to cast their cares on The Lord. I have seen the results. I have heard the testimonies. I am a living testimony myself. So, why am I still losing sleep once in a while? Why am I getting all melodramatic saying; "Oh, supernatural peace that I knew yesterday afternoon before my last spiritual attack, where for art thou?"

Yes, I woke up tired, so that means I woke up sensitive. Do you know those mornings? The mornings in which one coffee or tissue commercial can send your self- control packing and push your feelings into weepy mode. Yes friends, that was me this morning.

So, I did what I know to do. I grabbed my cup of Joe and I went to God as real and raw as I could be. I decided to start reading my Psalm and Proverb of the day and then before I knew it, God had me grab my journal. I can't even tell you how it happened; but, oh friend, it was miraculous. It was as if God decided to keep me up the night before so I would be too tired to keep my little butt in my bible study chair as He downloaded this book to me. I think He had you in mind too, He usually does when He shows me something. Our God is amazing at multi-tasking. He's ridiculously talented at burden bearing, and He's outstandingly detailed in His strategies.

God said; "Mo, you're fighting a secondary attack." I didn't quite understand what He meant until I started writing. He began to show me that even though I have learned how to overcome anxiety, the horrendously mammoth Goliath that took me much more than three stones and sling shot to conquer, I still had another flaming arrow aimed directly at me that I wasn't prepared for. He showed me that I haven't been winning this battle because I didn't even know I was in it.

Oh, I'm sure I've lost you now, right? You're like; "Oh, great, I got some spooky, kooky Christian author who thinks she talks to God as though He's in the room and she's lying on the therapy couch." Well, yes. That's exactly what book you have picked up. I am that girl. I'm the girl who lives in constant communication with The God of the Universe. I carry The Holy Spirit on the inside of me and He counsels me and comforts me day by day, minute by minute, second by second. You got it. That's who I am. I am the Jesus freak who lives each day grateful and thankful that He has shown me how to enjoy every second of my life and not allowed me to bow down to fear one more second that my old heart keeps beating. I am that mom who prays over her children each morning when they leave for school or work. I am that wife who lays hands on my husband's truck when it won't start knowing that our God can miraculously keep it running, and He does. I am that woman who stands up in front of women month after month at our regular women's event and says; not by might, nor by strength, but by the Spirit of God, I am healed.

Yes, I'm that author and I hope that knowing that, you will still give this book a chance because I can promise you one thing. I didn't write it, God did. I simply moved the pen, or I quickly moved my fingers to type what He told me to type. But, bear with me because I'm pretty sure if God writes something, it's going to be good.

He said; "You are fighting a secondary attack."

What is a secondary attack you ask? I asked God this same question. Turns out, it's emotions like that the big ugly G word called guilt. Guilt, is a secondary emotion. Secondary emotions are emotional reactions we have to other emotions. There are primary emotions, or what God showed me to be called, "premier attacks" and there are secondary emotions or in God's Words to me, "secondary attacks"

According to www.cornercanyoncounseling.com, Primary emotions are fairly simple to understand. They are your reactions to external events. Some precipitating event may cause you to experience emotion. Example: You may feel sad that someone hurt you or anxious about an upcoming test.

A secondary emotion is when you feel something about the feeling itself. Example: You may feel anger about being hurt or shame about your anxiety. The definition of the word Premier is; first in importance, order, or position; leading. Some synonyms are; leading, foremost, chief, principal, head, top-ranking, top, prime, **primary**, first.

The definition of Secondary is; coming after, less important than, or resulting from someone or something else that is primary. When God said: "You are fighting a secondary attack." I knew immediately what He was talking about. I understand why He kept me up that night. I knew the second that He said it, praise God that He was going to show me how to let go of my guilt problem once and for all. You see, I have studied the Word for so many years. He taught me how to fight my anxiety habit with the Word; but for some reason, I just kept feeling guilty all of the time, and couldn't seem to put the resources together to fight it until now.

Yes, God's timing is not our timing. He sits outside time and space. God doesn't watch the microwave clock and the clock on our phones the way we do. He is the author of time. It wasn't my time to be healed of guilt, or should I say; "Imagined guilt" until now.

If I were to say to you, this book is your ticket to get off of the guilt train, would you cash it in? If I were to say to you, there is work to be done. But, it is the kind of work that pays amazing emotional dividends

3

of peace and tranquility would you do the work? If I were to offer you practical and spiritual techniques that will teach you to hold up your shield of faith and extinguish the next flaming arrow aimed directly at you from the enemy of your soul, would you get out your armor and gear up? I hope your answer would be yes.

There is a premier fight. Yours may not be anxiety like mine is. It may be a different mental stronghold that you have to learn to break through the power of God's Word, prayer and The Name of Jesus. It may be a different habit or addiction. It may be a hurt that never quite healed right because you have not received the supernatural salve of The Holy Spirit yet. It may be a lack of forgiveness towards someone, and maybe that someone is even yourself.

 You know what your premier fight is. You know what your God-shaped hole is. Your God-shaped hole is that place in your heart that though you have tried and tried, it just can't seem to stay filled. It feels like life just keeps sucking it out like a vacuum. Well, the reason why nothing else seems to fill it is, that hole belongs to Jesus. He's the only one that can help us fight and win our premier fight.

He's it! He's the Father to the Fatherless and the husband to the husbandless. He's the healer to the sick. He's the giver of sight to the blind. The giver of hearing to the deaf, legs to the lame, words to the mute. He's our hope for the future, He's the healer or our pasts. He's the Mighty Counselor to the broken hearted and the Great Provider to the spiritually and financially broke. He's the peace that you have been desiring. He's the friend that sticks closer than family. He's the giver or every good and perfect gift. He's all of these, everything else you can think of; and when we are done listing that, He's just getting started.

He's Jesus and He's who you need to fight the premier fight and win. He's who you need to fight the secondary attack and win. There is a premier fight, and like it or not, it seems to be the thing that draws you the closest to God. That's how those premier fights are. They exist because we live in a fallen world and we face an enemy of our souls.

They exist because the devil; who has a plan for our lives to steal, kill and destroy us, he has used these ugly premier fights attempting to steal our peace, rob our joy and kill our testimonies.

However, God has taken that which the enemy has tried to use to take us down, sometimes our whole lives, and God has used these premier fights to draw us closer to Him. Our God is amazing! Our God has done exactly what Joseph said He would do in Genesis 50:20: " You intended to harm me, but God intended it for good to accomplish what is now being done, the saving of many lives."(NIV)

There is a premier fight that has to be fought first. If your premier fight is anxiety or fear, I pray that you work through my "Overcoming Anxiety" book first. If your premier fight is any other hurt, habit or painful trial that is obviously still unresolved, my advice is simple; learn to renew your mind daily in the Word of God as you seek wise counsel in obtaining your healing. The Word of God is truly our healing.

Jesus saved me, The Holy Spirit counseled me, and The Word of God healed me. It is God's will that you learn how to fight the good fight of faith and win your premier fight. It is my prayer that you allow this healing to happen. It truly is a choice. Make that decision today to fight and win.

The Next Arrow is your secondary attack you will have to conquer after you have learned to battle and win in the Premier attack, or fight. The next arrow coming is just as much a deliberate shot from the enemy of your soul to steal, kill and destroy as the premier attack was. The next arrow is shot directly at you by a devil who knows his days are numbered. Make no mistake he's ticked off that you have realized that it is for freedom that Christ died to set us free. That devil hates your pursuit of Godly things.

Friend, the next arrow is a flaming dart that can only penetrate you if your armor is off. The next arrow, most of the time, isn't even real. It's imagined. The next arrow may be guilt, and it's completely opposite of

God's will for your life. Whether or not this secondary attack is guilt, or anger or even jealousy, you need to understand that this arrow has been shot at you with such sneaky deliberate hatred, that you have forgotten that you are more than a conqueror. Please know, this arrow has been shot at you, but you are able to shield from it.

God said; "The Longer you fight the premier attack in your own power and not mine, the more real the next arrow feels." What we dwell on long enough becomes reality to us. Remember this as you begin this journey to healing with me. I'm probably going to say it over and over. "Not everything we feel, is real." "Not everything we feel, is real." Now, that's some good rhyming revelation there. That's a rhyme you can take into everyday life to help you stay in some peace and holiness. When we are talking about the secondary attack or emotion of guilt, much of the time the guilt that you are feeling isn't real.

When I am talking to a Christian brother or sister about guilt, I can say with even more confidence, "your guilt isn't real." How can I speak that over your life, not even knowing what sins you have committed in the past, or will commit in the future? I speak it with the authority of the Word of God that says; "as far as the east is from the west, so far has he removed our transgressions from us. Psalm 103:12

When Jesus died on the cross for our sins and junk and mess ups and boo boos and imperfections and trash, He died once for all, and when He said; "It is finished." He took our guilt upon Himself. We are not supposed to carry that guilt and condemnation anymore. When we have repented and made Jesus Lord of our lives, at that moment He took full responsibility for us and He justified us and made us Holy.

You don't feel holy? That's ok. Remember, not everything we feel is real. If God's Word says that my sins, making me feel so guilty, are washed away because of Jesus' sacrifice on the cross, and they are as far as the east is from the west, then even though I don't feel guilt free, I have decided that I am. You see, I trust the Word of God. I trust the heart of Christ. I trust God. I really don't trust my feelings which are a mess sometimes. They change daily and are affected by everything from too much coffee to hormones. Even though many days I feel guilty, I must remember that I am forgiven and justified.

The word justification actually means; "Just as if I never sinned." Wow, I love that word justification. It brings a natural perfectionist like me so much peace. Yes, even though we feel guilty that doesn't mean we are guilty. It's time that we take the control of our feelings back from the enemy. He has no authority over them. We belong to God. Let's make a decision today to let God heal us even we feel undeserving.

Are you tired of feeling guilty all of the time? I know I am. In the natural, I feel guilty:

When I see an injustice in the world and I think somehow I should be able to fix it.

When I struggle as a wife or as a mother.

When I think about how much older my kids are now, and how I probably worried a lot of their years away when they were little and I should have savored every second.

When I focus on the "would haves and should haves of life"

When I see someone hurting and my day is going well. I feel guilty for that joy sometimes.

When I have been attacked in my thinking with some type of temptation. Even when I fight it correctly and I crucify my flesh and renew my mind in the Word, the next emotion I usually feel is guilt about even fighting those thoughts.

Is this too real for you? Because I have to be real, so we can be healed. How about we step off of the guilt train once and for all and allow God to show us how to repel each one of the devil's next arrows he is aiming at us. I know I am ready to. I know God is ready for me to. It's time to send that devil packing. He's had enough time messing with my peace.

Jesus paid way too high a price for my freedom. Not today devil!

I'd love for you to join me in this endeavor to put the devil in his place once and for all. Throughout these chapters, I may get a little preachy. It's only because I love you, and I want to see you walk in the freedom Christ died for us to walk in. You have already noticed probably that I am as transparent as any author can get. I share my struggles. I share my insecurities. I share my weaknesses. I do this, because it breaks the enemy's strength and the truth sets us free. I have decided to stand for freedom. I have worn invisible shackles that were not mine to wear for too long.

I'm going to be sharing some journal entries from my blog on wordpress.com. Please feel free to follow me on my blog as it's another way we can march on to victory together, closely following Jesus and His Word. I do this so that you can get to know me better. I always love being able to picture the author of whatever book I'm reading in my mind's eye. I picture her sitting and typing from her keyboard. I guess it makes the words seem more authentic to me. The script then becomes more than words on a page. It becomes lessons the author has learned, the easy way and the hard way, and is now teaching them to me. I pray this book becomes that real for you.

More than a Conqueror

Posted on April 20, 2015 by momydlo

Wow, I woke up on fire today. I don't know if it's the amazing coffee I drank this morning or the fact that I adore when God strips back one more layer of my anxiety so I can share the advice with others. I just love when He guides my next step and then waits for me to jump.

I have been reading Isaiah. I love the book of Isaiah. I don't know how analytical people cannot just realize that there is absolutely no doubt the resurrection took place, because the prophetic words that were spoken of Jesus hundreds of years in advance, all took place. It's just the best history book ever written.

God has been keeping me in Isaiah 54 for quite a few days. I didn't really know why, but I have been experiencing fresh eyes and wisdom about things I have read plenty of times. That's the beauty of our living and breathing bibles.

In Isaiah 54:17 it says; "No weapon that is formed against you shall prosper, and every tongue that shall rise against you in judgment you shall condemn. This is the heritage of the servants of the Lord, and their vindication is from Me says the Lord." (MEV) We have heard this so many times, right? "No weapon formed against us shall prosper. I am more than a conqueror. I am the righteousness of Christ." We have heard these things, and we speak them like they are every day words as Christians, but do we ponder them in our hearts? Do we realize what God is trying to say to us? Do we have any idea the power in these truths? These are written for us! They are written so we know how to fight.

Do we understand that though God says; "their vindication is from Me." He says something right before that; "every tongue that shall rise up against you in judgment *YOU shall condemn. (*We are the you God is talking to!) We are the ones that have to tell the enemy who is throwing flaming darts of condemnation our way that we aren't putting up with his nonsense anymore. We have to fight a little. We can hear a zillion times we are more than a conqueror, but sometimes we don't even want to conquer at all. We sit back, worry, get anxious, let the enemy control our thinking; then we dwell on his lies long enough that he steals our joy at the least. Then... maybe if we call on enough Word and the name of Jesus just enough to get him to flee, we feel so crappy (Yes I said crappy) afterwards that we were attacked that way in our thinking; we let him tell throw his guilt bombs at us after; "oh, you have a terrible mind. Nobody thinks like you. Wow, what a mess you are."

You see, there is a primary attack we have to fight! We have to condemn the enemy the second he throws any irrational thoughts, temptations or fears our way. Then, after we have won the initial battle with The Word, the Name of Jesus and prayer, we have to stand our ground against the secondary attack of guilt that the devil will try to throw at us. We have to stand on the truth in knowing this; and please, hear me here, you are not crazy! The devil is not creative! He tempts us all to sin! Everyone gets terrible thoughts! You simply have to rebuke him and put him back in his place, and pursue holiness. We have to make a choice daily to choose God's thoughts and not the devil's! That's it!

My friend, God told me to be real, so people can heal! You are not crazy! You are more than a conqueror! But, you have to conquer! No more letting Satan think he has won. Fight him today with The Word. Then..."their vindication is from Me, says the Lord." I love you. That's why I'm real

Premier or Secondary Attack, We Need to Know How to Fight

Guilt is not the only secondary attack of the enemy. We are going to discuss a few of them in this book. There are many secondary attacks that are aimed at us from the enemy of our soul and they are fought the same way that we fight premier attacks, head on, with Jesus as our Defender and The Word of God as our sword. I promise, you don't have to feel tired already reading this, thinking, *great, I thought now that I'm a Christian I am supposed to live in peace, and you're telling me I have a lifelong fight to pursue.* Quite the contrary my friend. If you have not mastered how to fight spiritual warfare correctly, you are going to be fighting anyway. The difference is that without the correct tools, you won't have victory. I want to teach you how to fight and win. I want to teach you how to fight for the peace that Christ died for you to have. I want to show you how to grab onto that peace and never let it go. You see, we will fight; but learning to fight correctly, ensures that we fight and win and that peace is ours in Jesus' Name.

Fighting Premier or Secondary Attacks is a necessity. As Christians we fight a war called Spiritual Warfare. According to allaboutJesus.org, "Spiritual warfare exists in the unseen, supernatural dimension, where God is all-powerful and Satan is in revolt. As any Christian soon discovers, although spiritual warfare is unseen, it's absolutely real. The Bible speaks of spiritual warfare in many places, but most directly in Ephesians 6:12-13 where Paul speaks of putting on the full armor of God: "For our struggle is not against flesh and blood, but against the rulers, against the authorities, against the powers of this dark world and against the spiritual forces of evil in the heavenly realms. Therefore put on the full armor of God, so that when the day of evil comes, you may be able to stand your ground, and after you have done everything, to stand."

Spiritual Warfare is very real. 1 Timothy 6:12, teaches, "Fight the good fight of the faith. Take hold of the eternal life to which you were called when you made your good confession in the presence of many witnesses." I love this passage. First, we need to understand that this is the apostle Paul encouraging his disciple Timothy. He had just talked to Timothy about not being swayed by the love of money. He is explaining contentment to him, not saying that money is evil, but the love of money is evil. He is truly trying to keep him protected from that.

In the verse before he talks about fighting the good fight. He says, "But, you, man of God, flee from all of this, and pursue righteousness, godliness, faith, love, endurance and gentleness." He's trying to encourage Timothy to be aware of how he begins to feel about money, and pursue righteousness. This is obviously a decision that Timothy will have to make. He will have to flee from one, and pursue the other, which take a little bit of fighting.

This fighting is something that we as believers are familiar with. Paul was only talking about the love of money here. However we have so many other things that our flesh (our sin nature) will desire that is contrary to what the Spirit will desire. We will have to flee from the first, and pursue the things of the Spirit.

Spiritual warfare is very real. As modern day Christ followers we have to know how to fight. We have to learn to fight our flesh; we have to learn to fight the enemy; and we have to learn how to fight against being polluted by the world. We will fight premier attacks and secondary attacks. The only sure fire way to fight the enemy, and win is to fight according to The Word of God.

Often spiritual warfare begins in our thinking. The mind is a battleground that the enemy chooses to attack first. If the devil can get us thinking incorrectly, he can gain some ground in battle against us. It is up to us as authorized children of God to learn how to fight the enemy and win beginning with our thinking and moving forward to every area of our lives.

We battle premier and secondary attacks by renewing our minds in the Word of God and learning how to put on the full armor of God to fight and win. We fight premier and secondary attacks of the enemy by learning how to crucify our flesh daily. We must ingrain into our being the truths of God's Word, live according to them in our minds, our souls and our bodies. Sin is no longer our master. We serve righteousness now. Our victory starts and ends by renewing our minds and crucifying our flesh daily.

Real or Imagined?

I had a supernatural thing happen to me one day while I was doing housework. I was making my son's bed and as I was pulling up the covers I heard me say to myself, "Oh ya, God told me to research imagined guilt". Then, I stopped for a second and thought, *when did God tell me to do that?* I realized that The Holy Spirit had just told me, "Research imagined guilt."

After I finished making the bed, I went out to my computer and googled, "Imagined guilt." Guess what? It's a true thing. Many people suffer with feeling guilty for things that they have not done. The Holy Spirit was ministering to me as if to say, "Mo, let's get rid of some of this guilt that isn't yours to carry."

The dictionary defines the word guilt as a "feeling of responsibility or remorse for some offense, crime, wrong, etc., whether real or imagined." Just reading the dictionary's definition of guilt and seeing that some of our guilt is imagined, released my burdens in a major way. I was able to realize that just because I feel guilty, doesn't mean I am guilty. That is how detailed the beautiful Holy Spirit is. He needed me to see that guilt is real sometimes, and sometimes we are imagining it.

Say this out loud right now. "Just because I feel guilty, doesn't mean I am guilty." Oh friend, there are a few reoccurring themes in a lot of my teaching as a preacher. You will probably hear me say these things more than once if you ever hear me teach.

1) You have to renew your mind daily in The Word of God.

2) Your feelings are liars! They don't get a vote.

Just because we feel guilty, doesn't mean we are guilty. An over-active guilty conscience always second guesses its decisions and actions. When you struggle with a guilt complex it can make us highly self-critical.

Guess what is the underlying cause of an overactive guilty conscience? Fear.

Imagined guilt is based on irrational fear. Guess who hands us fear? Satan! We fear letting others down; we fear imperfection; we fear failure; we fear "messing this whole thing up." (That example is in quotes because I have heard the devil whisper that lie to me way too many times). These fear based emotions like anxiety are the premier emotions that lead to secondary emotions like guilt, whether it is real or imagined.

We have to remember something if we want to break free from the gripping hands of guilt and fear, 2 Timothy 1:7 says, "For God has not given us the spirit of fear, but of power, and love, and self-control." (MEV) Fear is not from God. He doesn't place fear in us. Fear is learned. It is acquired. It is taught. It is demonstrated in front of us. Fear is not part of our Spiritual DNA. Fear is what has been handed to us through life and lies.

Fear is the enemy's attempt to separate us from the perfect will of God for our lives. If Satan can lure us into fear, he can paralyze our faith and lead us into reliance on idols and defense mechanisms to find a bit of lasting peace in this life. If the devil can cause us to fear, he can take us away from trusting. Trusting God with our lives brings peace, and not trusting God with our lives brings fear. Say this to yourself 3times! Fear is not from God! Fear is not from God! Fear is not from God!

Do you want anything that isn't from God? I don't. God has my best interest at heart. God has your best interest at heart. God loves us. He is enamored with us. We are the apple of His eye. We are His children, His babies, His loved ones. God can't resist loving us. God is love. I only desire what God has for me, and nothing else.

If God has peace for me, I want it.

If God has joy for me, I want it.

If God has protection for me, I want it.

If God has health for me, I want it.

If God has wisdom for me, I want it.

I want everything that God has for me, and nothing that He doesn't. Fear is not from God, so I don't want it.

God's Word says, "Perfect Love casts out fear." 1 John 4:8. What casts out fear? Because I want that as well. The Word here says, perfect love, is what casts out fear. Well, what is perfect love? Perfect Love is Jesus Christ Himself. Jesus Christ is love. He is perfect Love. If the Word says, "Perfect Love casts out fear, and Jesus is perfect Love, then I would say, "Jesus casts out fear!"

When we fear. We need to remember that Perfect Love Jesus Christ lives on the inside of us because we are believers in Him. So, if Perfect Love is on the inside of us, taking up residency in our hearts, then where Perfect Love is, fear is not. "Perfect Love casts out fear." If fear tries to creep in, we must remember to simply allow Jesus Christ to cast it out.

In order to effectively relieve our burdens of real or imagined guilt in our lives, we have to address and eradicate the premier emotion of fear, before we can begin to touch our war with fear's ugly brother, guilt.

Fear has to be dealt with by learning how to cast down the unwanted emotion immediately, then replace it with the Word of God. I explain techniques on how to do this in my book, "Overcoming Anxiety, Your Biblical Guide to Breaking Free from Fear and Worry." We are overcomers in Christ and we can learn how to trust God with every detail of our lives. It takes time to learn how to trust at that level, but we are able to because we are believers in Jesus Christ.

The Word of God planted deep into our heart and called on whenever we are in fear, is the sustaining force that will catapult our faith to a trust level where healing happens. We must immediately take captive fear thoughts, cast them down, replace them with God's Word and then stand on that truth until peace comes. Peace will come. It is promised. God's Word says, "Do not be anxious about anything, but in everything through prayer and petition, with thanksgiving lift up your requests to God, and the peace that passes all understanding will guard your hearts and minds in Christ Jesus."

What does this peace that passes all understanding mean? That sounds pretty amazing right? Yes, it is. That basically means, you won't even understand why you feel that peace. It just happens. It's supernatural. It's released from the gates of Heaven into your soul. It's straight from God.

That peace is promised when we do what the verse says prior to it, we give everything to Him, through prayer and petition with thanksgiving. We have to first do the handing over of our junk, before we can receive the beauty of His peace. It's a perfect exchange. We are definitely on the blessed side of that exchange. We get to give God our struggles, our worries, our fears, our anxieties, and He gives us, peace. I don't know about you, but I've decided to take God up on that exchange and He's never let me down since.

Once we finally learn to trust God more than we fear, we can recognize where the enemy really doesn't have a lot of tricks up his sleeve. After we rebuke the fear, speak the Word, stand on the Word and see peace come, arm yourself friend, there is most likely another arrow coming. Hold up your shield of faith, because the next arrow is no doubt sitting in the devil's quiver, just waiting to be released. Most likely he's aiming at you next with a fiery dart of guilt. Gear up sister! Gear up brother! We can extinguish all of his flaming arrows. But we'd better have up our shield of faith.

The devil will try to come at you with lies of guilt, shame and condemnation. Maybe he will attack with jealousy or anger. Whatever the next arrow is, he's not going to be happy about your newfound trust in God and His Word and The Word's unyielding victorious power. He's probably going to start with some lie shots. He will most likely aim right at your Achilles heel. I promise he knows what all of ours are. If your soft spot where he gets you to fear is your children, that's most likely where he will attack you. If your soft spot where he gets you to fear is your health, that's most likely where he will attack you. If your soft spot where he gets you to fear is your finances, that's most likely where he will attack you.

Gear up! He's calculated. He studies us. He sees where we are weak. He's a lazy enemy and he isn't going to work hard hitting you when you feel strong. He is going to attack at your weakest areas.

But God has provided a way for us my friend. The answer is in 2 Corinthians 12:6-10, "But I refrain, so no one will think more of me than is warranted by what I do or say, or because of these surpassingly great revelations. Therefore, in order to keep me from becoming conceited, I was given a thorn in my flesh, a messenger of Satan, to torment me. Three times I pleaded with the Lord to take it away from me. But he said to me, "My grace is sufficient for you, for my power is made perfect in weakness." Therefore I will boast all the more gladly about my weaknesses, so that Christ's power may rest on me. That is why, for Christ's sake, I delight in weaknesses, in insults, in hardships, in persecutions, in difficulties. For when I am weak, then I am strong.

My friend, the answer is God's grace. God's grace is sufficient in our lives to handle anything that the enemy throws at us. God's power is actually made perfect in our weakness; because in our weakness, God pours out His grace, (his undeserved, unmerited favor), to completely equip us to fight the good fight of faith in any battle.

When the enemy extends his bow and releases that next arrow of guilt at us straight to our Achilles heel, we are able to stand firm and not be moved because of God's perfect and amazing grace poured over our situation. His grace is sufficient. Oh, my friend, His grace is sufficient.

Grace is the Key!

Posted on December 10, 2012 by momydlo

This morning I was watching "It's Supernatural" and Sid Roth had a guest on there talking about daily pursuing Holiness, and the false teaching that you can never fall from God's grace. It is quite obvious in scripture that God is serious about us pursuing holiness, and that we need not think that we can pray one prayer for salvation then live sloppy lives, and know that our home is secured in Heaven.

That true gospel cut right to my Spirit like The Word as a double edged sword, piercing bone and marrow. I have a true fear of the Lord, and of course the first thing I had to do was run to Him in prayer. I asked for His forgiveness for where I fall short, and asked Him; "How can I do it Lord? If sin is sin, and I think poor thoughts, then how do I pursue daily holiness?"

I asked Him if I needed to be praying in the evening more too. After all, I start out good in the morning. I work at pursuing holiness during the day, but then I mess up. I gossip, I think poor thoughts, I miss opportunities to love, and so much more. So, is that it Lord? Do I need to every night repent for where I messed up during the day? I just want to please you."

As I got in the shower. I felt God give me the answer. For some reason, God knows I love rhymes. It must be the poet in me. He said; "Stay in the race, relying heavily on GRACE!" That's it! I just can't give up. Jesus' blood covers my sins, but I just can never turn my back on that sacrifice. I can never forget the price that was paid. I can never stop telling others of that love. I have to stay in the race.

Yes, there will be some days that I limp, some that I need a ride, and some that I feel like running. But, that race is marked out for me, and I just cannot quit! After all, there is an amazing prize at the finish line, a forever home with Jesus!

Don't overthink it my friends. Stay in the race, relying heavily on grace.

How do we combat the Imagined Guilt?

We fight the imagined guilt that can torment us so drastically the same way that Jesus fought, with humility and authority. Right now I want to talk about the humility that is needed to understand why we have to fight this. We must humble ourselves and realize that our original bloodline that stretches all the way back to Adam and Eve has been contaminated with sin.

We are born into sin because of the original sin in the garden. We are born sinners. The second that we are born again, we become children of God and we are no longer sinners. We are the righteousness of God in Christ Jesus. Does this mean we will not sin? Heaven's no! Our old sin nature is dead, but there are remnants inside us that are aching to resurrect at any time. The only one that can resurrect sin in our bodies is us. We have the authority not to sin, but we must be humble enough to remember that our old sin nature is still there. Then we must walk in the authority we have as Christ followers to remind that sinful nature, "You're dead to us!"

Guilt and shame are not from God. Guilt and shame are of the enemy and of our old sinful nature. If we are dead to sin, we are dead to guilt and shame. The remnants in our memories of the guilt and shame of our past or the imagined guilt of our past have to be reminded that "they are dead to us."

Dead to Sin

Galatians 5:1 says; "It is for freedom that Christ has set us free. Stand firm then and do not let yourselves be burdened again by a yoke of slavery."

Here Paul is talking to the church in Galatia who have received Christ and been saved. However, they felt they needed to keep going back and following the old Jewish laws and traditions. In Galatians 4:8 he says; "Formerly when you did not know God, you were slaves to those who by nature are not gods. But now that you know God or rather are known by God, how is it that you are turning back to these weak and miserable principles?"

My friend, these Christians experienced freedom from the law by placing their faith, hope and trust in Jesus Christ. They no longer had to follow all of the hundreds and hundreds of stipulations, rules, offerings, and sacrifices over and over just to feel worthy to worship. They experienced the grace and peace and forgiveness of Jesus Christ, yet they started turning back to old ways and habits. Paul tries to urge them to stand firm and not be burdened again, Paul is speaking the same thing to us today.

But, may I step out and say, we do it with slavery to sin. We do it with guilt and shame and other emotions. We forget we have been set free, and we put the old noose back on and let the devil have the reigns. It is for freedom that Christ has set us free. We need to walk out that freedom and throw off Satan's sin that so easily entangles.

Let's look at Galatians 5:16-22-23: So I say, walk by the Spirit, and you will not gratify the desires of the flesh. For the flesh desires what is contrary to the Spirit, and the Spirit what is contrary to the flesh. They are in conflict with each other, so that you are not to do whatever you want. But if you are led by the Spirit, you are not under the law.

The acts of the flesh are obvious: sexual immorality, impurity and debauchery; idolatry and witchcraft; hatred, discord, jealousy, fits of rage, selfish ambition, dissensions, factions and envy; drunkenness, orgies, and the like. I warn you, as I did before, that those who live like this will not inherit the kingdom of God.

But the fruit of the Spirit is love, joy, peace, forbearance, kindness, goodness, faithfulness, gentleness and self-control. Against such things there is no law."

So, here Paul is displaying the differences in the fruits of the spirit and the acts of the sinful nature, and he starts right out with how to fight. He says, "So, I say, "live by the Spirit and you will not gratify the desires of the sinful nature."

We all admit we don't want anything to do with these ugly aspects of our sinful nature; sexual immorality, impurity, debauchery (which means; excessive indulgence in sensual pleasures), listen, I didn't even know what debauchery meant. I remember thinking, *"that name sounds bad. I don't want debauchery."*

Idolatry and witchcraft, hatred, discord (what's discord mean? strife, conflict, friction) Oh come on friend, I know we haven't mastered that one. I'm on Facebook. Jealousy, fits of rage, selfish ambition, dissensions (which means; strong disagreement; a contention or quarrels) hmm, I'm in women's ministry, so I surely know we still struggle with quarrels. How about Factions? A group of persons forming a cohesive, usually contentious minority within a larger group. 2. Conflict within an organization or nation, and envy, drunkenness, orgies and the like. Paul goes on to say; "I warn you, as I did before, that those who live like this will not inherit the kingdom of God."

Ok, well, I know dear reader that you're feeling really good now, right? I'm sure you're thinking, *"Well this is not good news."* I know, it's hard to read this, but, the truth is, our sinful nature is ugly. It is selfish, immoral and ugly. We must learn the way to overcome it. We not only have to overcome it. We have to destroy it.

Do you want to put your ugly flesh to death? I know that I do. Are you sick of drama and arguing, feeling guilty for impure thoughts, being tempted to pursue this world's stuff, greed and all of our fleshy fits? Are you sick of it? I am! I thank God I'm never left to a life without Holy Spirit leading me saying:

"Yes do that."

"No, walk away."

"Walk that off Mo!"

"Don't think on that."

"Be still, stop pacing."

"Eat this, not that"

"No coffee this afternoon Mo, you are anxious."

"Don't think that way about her."

"Let that go Mo, you can't control that."

"Stop worrying if she likes you. Are you ok if she doesn't?"

"You're not going to screw this all up."

"Rebuke him Mo in my name. Tell him to leave."

"Get in the Word. Put it in your mouth, say it to your heart."

"Stop listening to those lies. I won't let you fall. I'm here."

My friend, the sinful nature desires what is in conflict to the Spirit. Thank God we have Holy Spirit! We have Him! He's real you know? He is our Counselor, Guide, Comforter, Protector, and Deliverer from trouble. Holy Spirit is with us if we have made Jesus Lord. If you have Holy Spirit, you will be able to fight, and win.

But my friend, you need Holy Spirit. There's no drug, no therapy, no idol, no defense mechanism. There is nothing that this world has to offer that can help you fight spiritual warfare except The Holy Spirit and God's Word.

 If you are reading right now and you have never made Jesus Lord, when you have an enemy attacking you with tormenting emotions, you've pretty much brought a knife to a gun fight. You need Jesus!

If you have never accepted Jesus as Lord, today is the day. The Word says, "Today is the day of salvation." Do not wait until tomorrow, tomorrow is not promised. If you don't know how to accept Christ, it is simple. Right now, close your eyes and just from your heart pray these simple words right now, out loud,

"Jesus, I need You. I ask you to forgive my sins. I believe that You died on the cross for my sins and I believe God raised You from the dead. Come right now Lord Jesus and be The Lord of my life. I trust you and I accept you as Lord. Send your Holy Spirit to rule and reign in my life. I love you Jesus. Thank you for saving me." If you prayed this prayer, you are saved.

Trust that God has now sent The Holy Spirit to rule and reign in your heart. If you didn't have Jesus, you now have Jesus. No fear, my friend. Help has come. Holy Spirit has come. You have everything that you need now.

Now that you have invited Him in, The Holy Spirit has arrived, and He will equip you forever. The best part is that after He comes, He never leaves. He will never leave you, nor forsake you. He will teach you how to fight the devil. He will show you how to fight guilt and shame. He will teach you how to fight all premier and secondary attacks. The Holy Spirit is our Helper.

Do you want to know how to fight guilt and imagined guilt and shame and all sin? We fight the devil and win when we overcome evil with good. In order to do that, we have to know what is good. We've talked about our sin nature but the verse continues with, "But the fruit of the Spirit, (and spirit is capitalized because it's a person) which means, (the good things that come from Holy Spirit living on the inside of us) is, love, joy, peace, patience, kindness, goodness, faithfulness, gentleness, and self -control. Against these things, there is no law."

The truth is, if we want to be God fearing, fruit filled men and women for Christ, living out our testimonies in front of the world so we can point them to Jesus; then we must live according to the fruits of the Spirit. If we do, we will not break God's laws. It says, "against these things there is no law."

As Christians, we get hung up on not failing. I know I do. Are you like me? Do you worry about messing this whole thing up? We fight this fear and we fight the ugliness of our sinful nature by focusing on fruitful living, not on messing up. Does that make sense to you? That's how we fight and win. Colossians 3:1 says, "Since, then, you have been raised with Christ, set your hearts on things above, where Christ is seated at the right hand of God. Set your minds on things above, not on earthly things."

My friend, the key word here is set. Set your mind. We have to make a choice of what to think about. We have to choose to say no to that voice that wants to tell us everything that is wrong with us, everywhere we have messed up in the past and everything that we could possibly do in the future to mess up. We have to choose to say "No" to these thoughts, that just come so easily because we have thought them for so many years and we have to choose to set our minds on things above, as in Heaven. Things that God calls good.

We have to not only think about these things, but put them on. It says so in Colossians 3:12: "Therefore as God's chosen people. Holy and dearly loved (That's you friend, that's believers, that's God's kids) "As God's chosen people holy and dearly loved, clothe yourselves with compassion."

I want to talk a second about clothing yourself. We know how to dress. We know how to match our shoes to our shirt and our pants. We have to actually put on these things. God's telling us, clothe yourself with some other things. We have to put them on.

What things?

Compassion

Kindness,

Humility

Gentleness and patience

Bear with each other.

Forgive whatever grievance you have against each other.

Ok, who is bugging you today? Who do you need to forgive? Even if it is something little. I'm telling you my friend, do yourself a favor and forgive. Forgive as your Father forgave you.

"And, over all these things, (so now this one is important) Put on love." Here is something else we have to put on. *Oh, Mo are your saying, love doesn't just come to us easy?* Heck no!

Oh, there are some easy ones to love. Let's be real for a second, now if you have kids, you know some of them are easier. This doesn't mean that you love them any more than the more stubborn ones, it just means some are more laid back, they don't argue as much and honestly, they probably are the least like you. It's those kids that are just like us that make us have to walk away and say to ourselves; "put on love, put on love, put on love."

There are two key phrases here we that have to pull from in this passage, "clothe yourself and put on." We don't get out of the shower and walk out dressed, we put clothes on. We don't walk out into this sinful world clothed in love, peace, patience, kindness, goodness, gentleness, faithfulness, and self- control. We clothe ourselves in them. We put them on. We choose what's right.

We feel like holding a grudge, Holy Spirit says, "Forgive"

We feel like venting, Holy Spirit says, "Hold your tongue"

We feel like looking lustfully at other men, Holy Spirit says, "Guard your heart, it's the wellspring of life. Turn your eyes to me and honor your husband."

We feel like shouting from the rooftops about anyone we helped that day, "Holy Spirit says humble yourself, every good and perfect gift comes from above. Don't let the left hand know what the right hand is doing."

We feel like vindicating ourselves. It's not fair what they've done to us. People should know the truth," Holy Spirit says; "Be still. I am your vindicator. Whatever is done in the dark will be brought in the light."

We feel like quitting, because this fight to stay pure and lovely in an ugly world is hard, Holy Spirit says; Press on, finish the race, set your minds on things above." We choose that which is right and we do it.

1 Peter 3:8-15

Finally, all of you, be like-minded, be sympathetic, love one another, be compassionate and humble. Do not repay evil with evil or insult with insult. On the contrary, repay evil with blessing, because to this you were called so that you may inherit a blessing. For whoever would love life and see good days
must keep their tongue from evil and their lips from deceitful speech. They must turn from evil and do good, they must seek peace and pursue it. For the eyes of the Lord are on the righteous and his ears are attentive to their prayers, but the face of the Lord is against those who do evil. Who is going to harm you if you are eager to do good? But even if you should suffer for what is right, you are blessed. Do not fear their threats; do not be frightened. But in your hearts revere Christ as Lord. Always be prepared to give an answer to everyone who asks you to give the reason for the hope that you have. But do this with gentleness and respect,"

The first way we fight the devil is to overcome evil with good. Then what? Then we keep putting more on. We don't just put on the fruits of the Spirit. We put on our armor. The second way we fight the enemy is with The Armor of God.

Yes, we've heard our Christianese before; *The Armor of God; we are warriors; we are God's ambassadors; we are foreigners in this land; sent from Heaven.* Friend, we know what we've heard. However, we can't just be hearers of the Word. We have to be doers. We fight the enemy with the Armor of God.

The Armor of God

Ephesians 6:10-18

"Finally, be strong in the Lord and in his mighty power. Put on the full armor of God, so that you can take your stand against the devil's schemes. For our struggle is not against flesh and blood, but against the rulers, against the authorities, against the powers of this dark world and against the spiritual forces of evil in the heavenly realms. Therefore put on the full armor of God, so that when the day of evil comes, you may be able to stand your ground, and after you have done everything, to stand. Stand firm then, with the belt of truth buckled around your waist, with the breastplate of righteousness in place, and with your feet fitted with the readiness that comes from the gospel of peace. In addition to all this, take up the shield of faith, with which you can extinguish all the flaming arrows of the evil one. Take the helmet of salvation and the sword of the Spirit, which is the word of God. And pray in the Spirit on all occasions with all kinds of prayers and requests. With this in mind, be alert and always keep on praying for all the Lord's people."

Dear friend, we have to put on our armor! Let's break apart the armor and talk about it a bit. We have the belt of truth, buckled around your waist. Hmm, what does that say to me? I feel like we better know what we are believing because some of it is real and some is false. The truth is, the devil is a liar and he is going to work at getting you to believe his lies every day. That's all he has. He has no weapons but lies. You can only know this by reading your Word. Know your Word! It's the only truth. It's not half –truth. It's not some truth. It's complete truth. If what you are thinking or feeling doesn't line up with biblical truth then it is probably a lie.

The breastplate of righteousness needs to be in place. Dearest reader, we are not righteous because of anything we have done, not done or ever will do. We are made righteous when we accept Jesus Christ and His righteousness. His blood on the cross is the only thing that can make us righteous. Remember, that we were born sinners, and we needed a perfect sacrifice for our sins of the past, the present and the future. These are covered by the blood of Jesus Christ.

We cannot ever be righteous, (which means have right standing in front of a Holy God), without the righteousness of Jesus Christ covering us with His robe of righteousness. Friend, If Jesus is your Lord, you are the righteousness of God in Christ Jesus; so wear your breastplate of righteousness with honor. When the devil tells you that you are not worthy, you aren't forgiven and maybe you aren't even saved; send him back to the hell he crawled out of by saying out loud, "I belong to Jesus. I am His. I am righteous."

You must have your feet, fitted with the readiness that comes from the gospel of peace. Our feet are ready to walk out this walk because we know who we are because of this gospel. We can only walk in courage and strength and dignity when we know our Word. The Word of God is the gospel of peace. Jesus is the gospel of peace. Gospel means good news. Actually. It's too good to be true news. And, we have it! And, it helps us to be ready to walk it out.

We have a shield of faith, which extinguishes all the arrows of the evil one. We see here that the devil is going to send arrows your way. Your faith is your shield. You better hold up your faith shield and fight. If Satan tells you that you are unworthy, hold it up! If Satan tells you that you are still guilty, hold it up! If Satan tells you that something bad is getting ready to happen, hold it up! If Satan tells you, this Christian thing is all just a big hoax, you are just a speck of dust that is going to return to the ground someday and all of your testimonies and miracles are all coincidences, hold up your shield of faith and fight!

You better know what you believe. Your faith is your shield. The Word teaches that faith extinguishes the flaming arrows. Praise the Lord, they lose their strength and burn out the second they hit your faith shield.

Let's talk about the helmet of salvation. This world is dangerous. It is going to knock us down. We are going to have some bumps and bruises, and we may fall down on the concrete, but, because of our helmets of salvation, death has no sting. If God be for us, who can be against us. When we take our last breaths and God says, "Ok, my child, come home" It will have been our helmets of salvations that we will wear into glory.

Last but most assuredly not least, we have our Sword of the Spirit. This one we can charge the enemy with. With this piece of armor, we hold it out in front and run behind it. This is our Word. The Sword of the Spirit which is the Word of God goes ahead of us whenever we fight the good fight of faith.

Remember, Jesus fought the devil with the Word. We need to fight like Jesus fought. He said to the devil over and over, "it is written" and he quoted scriptures to get Satan to leave him alone. That devil has no defense against a warrior armed with the Word! If you want to fight and win, put on your armor and fight with the Word!

Verse 18 ends with "And pray in the Spirit on all occasions. My friend, we have to be praying. We have to be saying silent prayers, loud prayers, from your bible study chair prayers, in the isle at the grocery store prayers, dropping our kids off at school prayers, scared of what's happening in our world prayers and Lord, save my lost neighbor prayers. Pray in the Spirit on all occasions! We need to pray like we think we may drive Jesus crazy with how often we pray. Prayer is our lifeline. We better be praying people.

We have to fight sin and the devil by overcoming evil with good and we have to fight sin and the devil by putting on our armor. It is imperative that when we fight, we better be fighting the good fight of faith.

Paul tells Timothy in 1 Timothy 6:12, (and this goes for us as well) "Fight the good fight of the faith. Take hold of the eternal life to which you were called when you made your good confession in the presence of many witnesses." Make no mistake, we have to fight.

Reckon Yourself Dead to Sin

If you want to be victorious in fighting sin and the devil, you reckon yourself dead to sin! Or as I like to say, because I am a country girl, "I reckon I'm dead to this." We fight sin by remembering that we are dead to it! Romans 6:11 says, "In the same way, count yourselves dead to sin but alive to God in Christ Jesus." We have heard this before right? Count yourself dead to sin? But, how do we live this out? Well, we study first. So let's study this together. Let's figure out what Paul is saying here.

The verses in chapter 6 of Ephesians leading up to this are actually explaining grace. We have been saved by grace, so we don't have to worry about sinning anymore. We don't have to focus on sin, think about sin and worry about sin, because wherever there is sin present in our lives (because of the miraculous saving power of Jesus Christ) grace will always show up.

Paul makes sure that for his legalistic friends he explains, that doesn't mean we live sloppy, sin filled lives. He goes on to teach in Romans 6:1-10 "What shall we say, then? Shall we go on sinning so that grace may increase? By no means! We are those who have died to sin; how can we live in it any longer? Or don't you know that all of us who were baptized into Christ Jesus were baptized into his death? We were therefore buried with him through baptism into death in order that, just as Christ was raised from the dead through the glory of the Father, we too may live a new life. For if we have been united with him in a death like his, we will certainly also be united with him in a resurrection like his. For we know that our old self was crucified with him so that the body ruled by sin might be done away with, that we should no longer be slaves to sin— because anyone who has died has been set free from sin. Now if we died with Christ, we believe that we will also live with him. For we know that since Christ was raised from the dead, he cannot die again; death no longer has mastery over him. The death he died, he died to sin once for all; but the life he lives, he lives to God.

Then Paul says, "In the same way, count yourselves dead to sin, but alive to God in Christ Jesus. Therefore, do not let sin reign in your mortal body so that you obey it's evil desires."

The key here for us to learn from is in vs. 6: "For we know that our old self was crucified with him so that the body ruled by sin might be done away with, that we should no longer be slaves to sin." My friend, this helped me so much once I learned this next lesson. Please open up your spiritual ears to hear this next bit of wisdom that I have for you. *Just because we are still tempted to sin, doesn't mean we will sin.* Sin no longer is our master. We have a new master. His name is righteousness. We have everything we need in Holy Spirit to fight sin. So, when we are struggling with negative emotions, I am telling you, we have everything that we need in Holy Spirit to combat every one of them.

Heck yes, Satan will tempt us and yes, our old sinful nature will try to resurrect. But, the truth is, it's nailed to the cross. Jesus paid our penalty. Once we have reckoned ourselves dead to sin, it no longer is our master.

The truth is, you could be an earthly slave to someone and if that slave master dies and your earthly master no longer has dominion over you, until you realize that you can stop serving him, he could still control you from the grave. Your true freedom doesn't necessarily come when he dies, it comes when you realize he is dead and he can't control you anymore. The decision is yours.

Your freedom belongs to you in Christ. Your freedom to not sin and to choose righteousness and peace and tranquility and a life covered with the blessings of God, requires you to allow your slave master sin to die once and for all, but also, to stop letting him control you from the grave.

Right now say out loud, "I reckon I'm dead to this." You will have to say this to yourself over and over until you realize you one day, *wow, that doesn't control me anymore*. Whether it is guilt and shame, anger or fear or insecurity that is still trying to control you, whatever it is, I promise you, you are dead to it.

Tempted to cheat on your diet? Say, "I reckon I'm dead to this."

Tempted to wear something you shouldn't to get some attention? Say, "I reckon I'm dead to this."

Tempted to worry about tomorrow? Say, "I reckon I'm dead to this."

Tempted to fear the worst? Say, "I reckon I'm dead to this."

Tempted to hold a grudge against a sister? Say, "I reckon I'm dead to this."

Dear friend, we fight sin by considering sin dead to us. We fight any stronghold of the enemy or inclinations of the sinful nature by remembering that we are dead to them. We are dead to sin. We don't have to allow it to keep controlling us from the grave. Let your old slave master sin, die! He's already been crucified in Christ. He no longer lives. Jesus Christ now lives in you.

Let me show you something that I loved reading in Colossians. I love Colossians. The book of Colossians is rich. In Colossians 2: 20-23 Paul is urging the church in Colossae that Jesus is enough. His grace is enough. You have everything you need to fight sin in Him. Stop trying to make yourselves rules and rules and rules. You are making yourself crazy with these.

He says, "Since you died with Christ to the elemental spiritual forces of this world, why, as though you still belonged to the world, do you submit to its rules: "Do not handle! Do not taste! Do not touch!"? These rules, which have to do with things that are all destined to perish with use, are based on merely human commands and teachings. Such regulations indeed have an appearance of wisdom, with their self-imposed worship, their false humility and their harsh treatment of the body, but they lack any value in restraining sensual indulgence."

Here's the thing, thinking about how not to sin, focusing on not sinning, not sinning, not sinning, what are we thinking about? Sin! Paul says in vs. 23, "Such regulations have an appearance of wisdom, but they lack any value in restraining sensual indulgence." When we set out to try to be sin avoiders, what do we end up doing? Sinning, because our minds are focused on sin. We have to reckon ourselves dead to it.

We need to say, "I'm dead to that." Let it go, then focus on what God wants us to focus on. These things are in Matthew 6:33-34, "But seek first His kingdom and His righteousness, and all these things will be added to you. So do not worry about tomorrow; for tomorrow will care for itself. Each day has enough trouble of its own."

Precious reader, we have to be righteousness minded. We have to be Heaven minded. Remember, we have to set our minds on things above. Jesus tells us to think about the Kingdom and think about and seek righteousness. Sin will care for itself, you're dead to it. Next time you are tempted to bow down to imagined guilt or shame, say, "I'm dead to this, and alive to righteousness." Then focus on the Kingdom.

I reckon I'm dead to sin! We can wear our armor proudly and fight the good fight of faith. We can do this because we are dead to sin and alive in Christ Jesus. Yes, being alive in Christ is where our peace comes from, it's where our freedom reigns.

I'm Not Who I Used To Be!

Posted on June 7, 2016 by momydlo

I bet people who went to High School with me are amazed that I am in full-time ministry. Here's the truth; I was not that nice in school. I was selfish, self-centered and very insecure so I didn't always treat people the way I should have. I was a mean girl! Here's the good news; I'm not who I used to be. I am a new creature in Christ.

I didn't have Christ in High School. It wasn't until I was a young mother that I accepted Jesus Christ as my personal Savior. I was god of my own life and well, that sort of existence didn't produce much good fruit. But God!!!!!!

After I accepted Christ, God filled me with His Spirit and since then, I have learned to crucify my old flesh and renew my mind every day to the truths in God's Word so that I could learn to become all that God wants me to be. Thank you Jesus that my Spirit is already there. But, my soul and my body still have a long way to go. Thank God that our God is patient with us.

I was reading in Galatians 1 today. I found a scripture that Paul is speaking to the church in Galatia and it made me say; "YES!" Paul is telling of the saving, restoring and faithful work that God is doing in and through the life of a man who once was a Christian-killer. Verse 1:22-24 reads; "I was personally unknown to the churches of Judea that are in Christ. They only heard the report: 'The man who formerly persecuted us is now preaching the faith he once tried to destroy.' And they praised God because of me."

I thought about this message Paul was preaching and I thought; "*You are so awesome God!*" *Only Jesus Christ would decide to use the man who once was a terrorist and a huge threat to the faith, to be the one man that writes over 75% of the New Testament. ONLY GOD!*

Think you have done too much evil to be used by God? Think you are

36

beyond God's ability to save and restore? Think God doesn't want to use you? Wrong! If God can use Paul and if God can use Mo, He is able to use you. You aren't who you used to be.

That Lying Devil and Our Stinkin Thinkin

Our dinner table conversation tonight was probably a little different than many households. At the dinner table, our family always prays then does our "High" and our "Low" of the day. But, tonight we got deep. Tonight we talked about spiritual warfare. My 13 year old started sharing about some poor thinking that he was fighting today. He shared how he heard the devil talk to him as he was walking down the hallway to his science class, "Why don't you just keep walking and walk off the campus." He said, "Mom and Dad, I knew that was the devil talking to me. I realized it and I immediately thought about how much trouble I would get in, and how disappointed everyone would be with me, so I told the devil to shut up and I just went straight to science."

I told him how proud I was of him for his honesty and his openness. I also told him how completely thankful I was that he realized who was whispering to him. You see, my husband and I have openly explained to our kids that the voices that they hear tempting them to do right and wrong, are very real. We have taught them that they have a source and they need to know what those sources are, so that they can walk in the Godly authority they have as a Christians and live free.

I have to admit, after dinner, as I was cleaning up the dishes, I thanked God for the peace that my children are able to walk in because of the transparency and honesty and truth that we have incubated in our home. We share things that we get right and we share things that we get wrong. We speak it and we break the enemy's strength over us.

I'm so grateful to God that He said to me years ago, "Mo, you have to be real, so others can heal." I thank God that I was able to teach my children to fight the good fight of faith. Their peace and their ability to protect their peace and walk in holiness and reverential fear, is worth a lifetime that I struggled before knowing the truth. Yes, there truly is nothing better than seeing my children know the truth, stand on it, and live victoriously.

In John 10:10, Jesus warns the disciples and us about the devil's plan for our lives. "The thief comes only to steal and kill and destroy; I have come that they may have life, and have it to the full" Right here we see Satan's three goals that he has for us, to steal from us, kill us and destroy us. Well, that's comforting isn't it? I know that may not be easy to think about, but take heart, Jesus finishes up that statement by letting them know, "I have come that they may have life, and have it to the full."

Why must we know the devil's goals to steal, kill and destroy us? Doesn't it set ourselves up for fear? No, it protects us. Jesus warns them for their own good, and for ours; not to make us nervous, but so that we may be on our guard and protect ourselves from his schemes. He tells them this, and it is recorded in the Word to protect and prepare us. That is just how we have prepared our children for battle. Proverbs 4:7 says, "**The beginning of wisdom is this: Get wisdom. Though it cost all you have, get understanding**"

We have to understand how Satan works, so that we are not ignorant of his schemes, and to protect ourselves from him by the power of the Word, the Name of Jesus and by exercising our authority by trusting in both of these in order to stay protected in every way.

Satan attempts to fulfill his plan in destroying us by whispering lies to us. He is a liar and he has been since the beginning. We also know this because Jesus taught us this as well. John 8:44 says, "**He was a murderer from the beginning, not holding to the truth, for there is no truth in him. When he lies, he speaks his native language, for he is a liar and the father of lies.**

If Satan can get us to think about these lies, we can begin to believe his lies and we fall right into his destructive plan. It is imperative then, that we understand his schemes, learn to decipher his voice and actually develop our confidence in telling him to leave in The Name of Jesus, so that we can be completely safe.

His lies are one of his evil flaming arrows. He shoots deception at us daily. There is no method to how he works. He will strike sometimes when we are alone. He will strike in the middle of a crowd. He will strike in the middle of the night, the day, you name it. We cannot ever expect to be immune to his lies. We simply have to know how to distinguish them, then extinguish them with truth.

The enemy speaks contrary to the Word of God. He is a counterfeiter and he sets himself up against the Word of God to create strongholds in our minds, in hopes of getting us to succumb to temptation, habits, or fears. It is really easy to know when the devil is lying to you, if you know The Word of God. If you do not know The Word, you are susceptible to his attacks. If you do know scripture and you have hidden the Word in your heart, you have all the protection that you need to fight the good fight of faith and win.

When he lies, he then tries to get us to take the bait of his lie. He wants us thinking about it. Sin starts in our thinking. If our thinking is a mess, our lives usually end up a mess. If our thinking is good, our lives are usually going well. Proverbs 23:7 says, "For as he thinketh in his heart, so is he."(KJV)

If the devil can get us thinking about something negative or destructive, that is his first step. After he gets us thinking about it, he is hoping our thinking will continue and it will turn into contemplation and reasoning. If our reasoning begins spiraling into a negative direction, the devil is winning.

The Word says in Isaiah 1:18, "Come, let us reason together says The Lord." When we reason out things, it needs to be with the help of The

Holy Spirit, otherwise we can get ourselves into trouble with over-thinking and over-reasoning negative situations.

If we think about something too long, whether it is a good thing, or a bad thing, our brains start making memories of that thought and it begins to feel real, whether it is or not. The truth is, the longer we linger on a thought, the more real it becomes to us, even if it isn't real.

Our minds are amazing and intricate things. Our God is the ultimate Creator. He made us with such extra-ordinary detail. However, the devil also knows that about us, and he will try to use it against us, by trying to get us to take his bait. If he can get us to think a negative thought long enough, it can become dangerous.

It is imperative in spiritual warfare that we recognize immediately when we are thinking something that we shouldn't, believing something that we shouldn't or even pondering something we shouldn't. Once we recognize this, we have to take that thought captive and rebuke it in Jesus' Name.

2 Corinthians 10:5 New International Version (NIV)

"We demolish arguments and every pretension that sets itself up against the knowledge of God, and we take captive every thought to make it obedient to Christ."

If the thought that we are thinking is not obedient to Christ and His Word, we must arrest it and replace it with the truth. If we do not do this quickly, the enemy can gain some control in our thinking. We are responsible for every thought we think. We must wage war against the enemy by not only working to rebuke his lies and resist meditating on them, we also must practice thinking God-honoring thoughts.

Our first step is to recognize that we are being set-up by the enemy.

Our second step is to make a decision that we are not his toy.

Our third step is to say, "It's settled, I am able to resist this thought."

Then, the fourth step is to change your stinkin thinkin into God honoring thoughts.

God honoring thoughts

Philippians 4:8 New International Version (NIV)

"Finally, brothers and sisters, whatever is true, whatever is noble, whatever is right, whatever is pure, whatever is lovely, whatever is admirable—if anything is excellent or praiseworthy—think about such things."

So, what are God honoring thoughts and how do we train ourselves to think them? God honoring thoughts line up with The Word of God. God honoring thoughts are about loving God, loving people and making disciples. God honoring thoughts are centered on loving people the way we want to be loved. God honoring thoughts are bathed in thankfulness, gratefulness and joy. God honoring thoughts give us peace. When we are focused on love, joy, thankfulness and other thoughts that line up with God's Perfect Spirit, we are able to stay in peace. We are able to resist the devil's schemes and we are able to stay in God's perfect will for our lives.

I've known this scripture Philippians 4:8 by heart for years. It has helped me to decipher which thoughts I am supposed to take captive, arrest and make obedient to Christ. This scripture has helped me to capture the thoughts that I have thought about that are not God honoring. Lately, God has been showing me that I am still a step behind.

You see, God has been calling me to take more authority in my thinking. He has called me stay one more step ahead of the devil and his schemes. Besides calling me to arrest and capture the negative, destructive thoughts and make them submit to God, He is now asking me to choose to block those negative, destructive thoughts from ever entering; because there are too many God honoring thoughts going on in my brain to make room for Satan to work.

God spoke to me about two weeks ago in my worship time, and said, "It's your imagination that I want you to control." You see, I thought I was doing that by recognizing when the enemy is at work in my thinking and taking authority. But, God showed me that even the mediations of my heart need to be more honoring to Him.

Psalm 19:14 King James Version (KJV)

Let the words of my mouth, and the meditation of my heart, be acceptable in thy sight, O LORD, my strength, and my redeemer."

This Psalm spoke so loudly to me that day in worship and quiet time with The Lord. God was saying, "Mo, let's get your mediations acceptable." I repented in tears and wept before God asking Him for forgiveness.

The truth is, God knows our thoughts before we think them. He knows the words that are going to come out of our mouths before we speak them. He knows what we are thinking and I am 100% sure God was not honored by my thoughts that day, and for many days before. Oh friend, I had been battling in my thinking. I had been casting down poor thoughts. I had been taking captive thoughts that were not God honoring and I had been replacing them with truth. But, I hadn't gone into the battle in my thinking prepared to win. I was simply surviving.

God doesn't want us just surviving. He wants us thriving. He wants victory for us. Rebuking the enemy every two seconds and having to cast down poor thoughts every other minute isn't thriving, it's surviving. God showed me that there is a better way.

We thrive in spiritual warfare, by choosing God honoring thoughts. Not choosing God honoring thoughts after the attack, but before the battle begins. Choosing to think on the things of Heaven and not things of Earth before the attack, puts us one step ahead of the enemy. Choosing to think about Jesus and His love, puts us one step ahead of the enemy. Choosing to think about God's Word puts us one step ahead of the enemy. Choosing to think about love, joy, peace, patience, kindness, goodness, faithfulness, gentleness and self-control puts us one step ahead of the enemy. Choosing to think on these fruits of the spirit, choosing to think on Heavenly, eternal things, before the enemy can plant a negative thought in our minds, puts us one step ahead of the enemy.

How do we do this? We make an effort. First thing we must do when we wake up in the morning is to say, "Thank you God." What do we thank Him for? We thank Him for everything, starting with God giving us another day here on Earth. We go to God in thankfulness for everything good that we can think about. We can actually create a thankfulness journal so that we are not only speaking the thankfulness to God, we are recording it to go back and look at when we need it the most. We begin our days thanking God, we continue our days thanking God, and as the day progresses, we find more and more things that we realize are blessings, that we took for granted so many times before, and we thank Him for those things as well.

After we start in thankfulness we then move into Worship. We begin to tell God how amazing He is. We lift up His Name. We glorify Him. We bless Him and we speak out loud to God telling Him how much we love Him and how happy we are to serve Him. This could go on for a while. Worshipping and honoring God isn't a quick little box to check off your list. We are supposed to live lives of worship. We are supposed to Hallow His Name just like the Lord's Prayer teaches us to do.

Next we go straight to the Word. The Word needs to be read, spoken, written, and meditated on. We need to roll scriptures over and over in our minds, pondering them and asking God how to relate them to our everyday lives. The Word is supernatural. It will come alive to you differently every day. The same passage that you read yesterday can give you a complete new revelatory meaning today. We simply must decide that God's Word is our compass and guidebook for our lives and that we are humbly going to do whatever it says to do in any area that we encounter and are living out each day.

Thankfulness, Worship and study, produces God honoring thoughts. Now we need to pray that God protects these thoughts in our minds and we need to ask God to guard our thoughts from the enemy. Prayer changes how we live and move and behave. We cannot forget that prayer is our lifeline. Prayer is how we communicate with The Father, through the Name of Jesus and how we allow Holy Spirit to guide us into all righteousness and holiness.

Yes, we have to take captive every thought that comes in our minds. Yes, the enemy will sneak in some doozies. Yes, sometimes the devil will beat us to the punch. It's in those times that we must begin fighting the good fight of faith and kicking the enemy out of our thoughts. But, for the most part, choosing to think on whatever is true, whatever is noble, whatever is right, whatever is pure, whatever is lovely, whatever is admirable, excellent or praiseworthy, beforehand, will put you on an elevated battle ground against Satan and will secure your victory. We must choose to think about things God wants us to be thinking about. We don't have to fall prey to thinking about whatever thought falls into our minds. We must make our minds submit to us. We must choose our thoughts. We must be pro—active to be productive. We are called to walk in victory, not just survival.

Humility and Authority

1 Peter 5:6-10 (NIV)

Humble yourselves, therefore, under God's mighty hand, that he may lift you up in due time. Cast all your anxiety on him because he cares for you. Be alert and of sober mind. Your enemy the devil prowls around like a roaring lion looking for someone to devour. Resist him, standing firm in the faith, because you know that the family of believers throughout the world is undergoing the same kind of sufferings. And the God of all grace, who called you to his eternal glory in Christ, after you have suffered a little while, will himself restore you and make you strong, firm and steadfast.

Humble Yourselves

When people ask me, "Do you really not worry about anything anymore?" I usually say, "I'm human. We live in a fallen world. Of course I still *feel* fear sometimes. I just don't bow down to it anymore." That's the truth right there. That's my testimony in a nutshell. I'm a hot-mess too far from Jesus. Yes, I still feel fear. I am human. I just don't let fear control me anymore.

I have learned that the biggest battles in life have to be fought with humility and authority. It is that way in our premier fight against anxiety or whatever your premier fight is, and it is that way in the next arrow aimed at us of guilt. The best way to defeat any spiritual adversaries foreign or domestic, is in humility and authority.

One of my favorite things to do is listen to the bible on my phone. I have a speaker in my kitchen that I will plug my phone into and I pump that baby through the house so loud and strong that I can clean each room from back to front, throw in laundry, load the dishwasher and fill the dog's water bowl, all while studying scripture.

I love to speak the words that I know out loud along with the text. Sometimes, I have to admit, I probably sound like we do in the car when we don't quite know the words to a song, but we sing along loud and freely. You know what I mean. Come on. You do it. I see you at stop lights. We can't help it. Something joyful happens to us when that one favorite song comes on the radio and we crank that baby up and belt it out. It's like we can picture ourselves like Celine Dion on stage at Rockefeller Center.

That's how much I love listening to scripture and quoting it along with the app as I am going about my chores and daily routines, and let me tell you, the book of James and 1st and 2nd Peter, wow, those are a couple of my favorites. I think that maybe those are some of my battle books. What do I mean by that? I mean, when I find myself in the middle of a spiritual battle, you better believe I start reciting some Peter and James.

1 Peter 5:6 starts out with humble yourselves. Well, that's a sermon series all of its' own. Humble yourselves. Why do we have to humble ourselves? I'm going to answer that question with a different question. *In our spiritual battles in life like your premier and secondary attacks, working through them on your own, how's that working for you?*

I can't answer for you but I can answer for myself. I am a hot-mess without Jesus, period! Humility is our first weapon that we must obtain for our combat equipment or battle gear against the flaming arrows and fiery darts of the enemy. I'm hearing the Spirit tell me, to dig in here so, I have to go here right now, bear with me.

Do you not believe that you have an enemy? Well, whether you believe it or not, you do. Here are some scriptures proving this to be true.

- Matthew 4:1: Then Jesus was led by the Spirit into the wilderness to be tempted by the devil.

46

- Hebrews 2:14: Since the children have flesh and blood, he too shared in their humanity so that by his death he might break the power of him who holds the power of death—that is, the devil
- Luke 10:17-19: The seventy-two returned with joy and said, "Lord, even the demons submit to us in your name." He replied, "I saw Satan fall like lightning from heaven. I have given you authority to trample on snakes and scorpions and to overcome all the power of the enemy; nothing will harm you.
- John 8:44: You belong to your father, the devil, and you want to carry out your father's desires. He was a murderer from the beginning, not holding to the truth, for there is no truth in him. When he lies, he speaks his native language, for he is a liar and the father of lies.
- Ephesians 2:1-2: As for you, you were dead in your transgressions and sins, in which you used to live when you followed the ways of this world and of the ruler of the kingdom of the air, the spirit who is now at work in those who are disobedient.

Scripture proves over and over the fact that we have a real and true enemy of our souls. He's not a storybook character with a pitchfork and horns. He's as real as the nose on our face. He's not our friend and he is no joke. He hates us. His plan is our downfall. His schemes are cunning. His plan is our destruction. He's ugly. He's Satan and he's real.

We war against a real enemy. He has legions of demons at his disposal to do his bidding, to work on destroying our lives. I could venture to guess that one of the devil's most annoying truths that he has had to face is that when we give our lives to Christ and make Him Lord, the enemy loses any control in our lives. He not only loses control, He has lost our eternal souls when we die. Our eternal destinies are now sealed and protected by The Holy Spirit. We have become citizens of Heaven and we are no longer slaves to sin. We become slaves to righteousness.

The devil has everything to lose and nothing to gain when our lives are centered on Christ. So, quite honestly, it ticks him off so he uses everything he has to get us to misunderstand our authority and privileges, while here on earth as believers. He lies, cheats and steals to get us to forget who we are and Whose we are. That is why it is important that we understand how to decipher his voice and his tactics in our lives so we can stand against them and stand strong in The Lord.

I'd like to stop giving the devil any more press now, if you don't mind. The quicker that you realize that you are in the middle of a battle and it is not against flesh and blood that you are fighting, the quicker you will see your healing quickly appear.

Battle Gear

How can we fight the enemy, now that we know we actually know that we have an enemy? Humility is our first piece of ammunition in this fight against the devil's schemes. When preparing for our secondary attack of guilt, humility is key. The Word says in 1 Peter 5:6, "Humble yourselves, therefore, under God's mighty hand, that he may lift you up in due time."

Why must we humble ourselves first? The simple answer is, pride comes before the fall. It's biblical and it's all together true. When we think that we can conjure our way out of the premier and secondary attacks of the enemy, we are deceived. We need God's help. We need His supernatural light shone on our weaknesses and our strengths, our areas that we believe lies, and our natural inclinations

We need humility, as a soldier in God's army. Proverbs 15:33 says "humility comes before honor." Humility encourages us to stop relying on dead tactics and to start reaching out for Jesus' help. Humility gets us to stop trying to fight the devil and his temptations alone. Humility helps us learn to say, "His grace is sufficient for me."

While I was meditating on humility I felt myself getting a little tired. I closed my eyes for a few minutes to take an afternoon rest and God showed me this acrostic.

HOME (H-O-M-E)

Humility comes when we

Obey our

Maker and Master's

Entrance into every area of our lives.

You see, when we truly make Jesus Lord of our lives and He takes up residency in our hearts, it is to our Father's glory and our benefit for us to stop shutting Him out from certain areas of our hearts. We must give God total control, not just access to the areas that we say that He is welcome.

The word lord means boss. When we ask Jesus to be Lord of our lives, we are supposed to be making Him boss. He isn't supposed to be the co-pilot, He is supposed to be behind the wheel. Pride keeps Jesus in the passenger seat. Humility says, "She's all yours Jesus. Have your way."

Only when we can truly humble ourselves can we become strong enough to fight the enemy head- on in any attack that he challenges us in. 1 Corinthians 1:25 says, "For the foolishness of God is wiser than man's wisdom, and the weakness of God is stronger than man's strength."

We are stronger than we can ever be in the natural when we humble ourselves before God and trust in His plan and provision for our lives. When it comes to attacks from the enemy, we are the strongest we can ever be when we realize we need God to fight for us. 2 Corinthians 12: 7-10 reads; "To keep me from becoming conceited because of these surpassing great revelations, there was given to me a thorn in my flesh, a messenger of Satan, to torment me. Three times I pleaded with The Lord to take it from me. But He said to me, "My grace is sufficient for you, for my power is made perfect in weakness." Therefore I will boast all the more gladly about my weaknesses, in insults, in hardships, in persecutions, in difficulties. For when I am weak, then I am strong."

Can we just read that last part together a couple times and allow it to roll over in our minds?

"For when I am weak, then I am strong."

"For when I am weak, then I am strong."

"For when I am weak, then I am strong."

That's a little different than what our feelings tell us. That's a little different than what the world tells us. That's a little different than what self-help psychology tells us. The world and it's "believe-in-yourself" mentality and our feelings, all lie to us and tell us that if we feel weak that is bad. The world will encourage us to medicate ourselves to get stronger or to do something that makes us feel better temporarily, so we don't have to feel this way. The world after all, is all about our feelings. Then, this word of scripture in 2 Corinthians says, "When I am weak, then I am strong." What is the Apostle Paul talking about? He is saying that in our weakest of human situations, when maybe all we can do is muster up enough strength to say, "God, I need You. I can't do this alone", humility happens, God takes over, and strength comes.

That's it! Humility comes before honor, pride before the fall. Humility opens up the door for God's hand to intervene. Humility teaches us that God is God and we are not. Humility reminds us that we are merely humans that are blessed and empowered through a personal relationship with The God of the Universe. Humility doesn't make us weak. Humility makes us strong.

Humility says:

I've done all I can do on my own. Now I have to trust.

I have to:

Trust in the Name of Jesus

Trust in the Word of God

Trust in the Blood of Jesus to wash away my sin

Trust in the Holy Spirit's counsel and help

God honors humility. He loves a humble heart. I believe it makes The Lord happy to see us humble, because humility is the opposite of pride. The Pharisees (The religious teachers of the law) were a proud bunch and they seemed to be some of the only people who truly annoyed Jesus.

Humility brings us to the trusting part of our fight against any attack of the enemy. Not trusting in ourselves, but trusting in God. Humility requires faith. We have to humbly submit to God knowing that when Jesus said, "It is finished" on the cross, our victory was finished as well.

Luke 18:9-14

The Parable of the Pharisee and the Tax Collector

"To some who were confident of their own righteousness and looked down on everyone else, Jesus told this parable: "Two men went up to the temple to pray, one a Pharisee and the other a tax collector. The Pharisee stood by himself and prayed: 'God, I thank you that I am not like other people—robbers, evildoers, adulterers—or even like this tax collector. I fast twice a week and give a tenth of all I get.'

"But the tax collector stood at a distance. He would not even look up to heaven, but beat his breast and said, 'God, have mercy on me, a sinner.' "I tell you that this man, rather than the other, went home justified before God. For all those who exalt themselves will be humbled, and those who humble themselves will be exalted."

Looks like it's better to be a tax collector than a Pharisee!

Let's Follow Jesus' example of humility

Philippians 2:5-11 (NIV)

"In your relationships with one another, have the same mindset as Christ Jesus: Who, being in very nature God, did not consider equality with God something to be used to his own advantage; rather, he made himself nothing by taking the very nature of a servant, being made in human likeness. And being found in appearance as a man, he humbled himself by becoming obedient to death— even death on a cross! Therefore God exalted him to the highest place and gave him the name that is above every name, that at the name of Jesus every knee should bow, in heaven and on earth and under the earth, and every tongue acknowledge that Jesus Christ is Lord, to the glory of God the Father."

Remember the old phrase WWJD? What would Jesus do? It was on bumper stickers, tee-shirts, bracelets, you name it. The question is, have we written it on the tablets of our hearts? That is the goal. We are to strive daily to look, act, live, love and be more and more like Jesus every day. It should be everyone's goals to live Christ honoring, Christ following lives. That's what Christ followers do, they follow the example of Christ.

If you are ever going to copy anyone, copy Christ. If you are ever going to have a role-model, make it Christ. If you are ever going to emulate anyone, make it Jesus Christ. We need to practice humility like Christ practiced humility.

The Word says, "He humbled Himself and became obedient to death, even death on a cross." He didn't consider equality with God as something to be grasped when the truth is, Jesus Is God! He is God the Son, yet He still understood that He had to submit to the leadership of God the Father. If anyone had any reason for being a little full of himself, it could have been Jesus, but He never was. Jesus is the epitome of humility.

Jesus said; "The Son of Man did not come to be served, but to serve."(Matthew 20:28 NIV) He understood His role in serving Father God in humility and total honor. Jesus' humility should be our ambition and intention.

Did the humility of Jesus make Him weak? It is quite the opposite. In Philippians 2:8 we read that "He humbled Himself by becoming obedient to death, even death on a cross." Then only one verse later, his humility was rewarded by The Father. "Therefore God exalted him to the highest place and gave him the name that is above every name, that at the name of Jesus every knee should bow, in heaven and on earth and under the earth, and every tongue acknowledge that Jesus Christ is Lord, to the glory of God the Father."

Jesus' humility exalted Him to the highest place. Jesus' humility gave Him the Name that is above every name, that at that name every knee will bow someday in heaven and on earth and under the earth. Jesus' humility now causes every tongue to acknowledge that Jesus Christ is Lord. Jesus' humility brings glory to God the Father. Humility is the opposite of weakness. Humility opens the door for God's power to be made perfect.

As I was hanging up clothes the other day, I was meditating on God showing me why the second attack of guilt from the enemy is fought with humility and authority. I love that about God. He can talk to us while we are doing chores, while we are sitting in car rider line picking up the kids, while we are grocery shopping, or at work. God speaks to us day and night, morning, afternoon and evening, while we are sitting or on our knees, while we are jogging or laying down. He speaks to us all of the time.   We simply must have on our spiritual ears to be listening for His voice. We have to learn to turn down the volume of all the distractions in order to hear.

I asked God, "Why do we fight the devil with humility and authority?" Then, before I knew it, I heard. "That's how my Son fought the devil." I ran to the quickest piece of paper I could find and I wrote, "Jesus humbly died on a cross, and Jesus boldly and with authority took authority over Satan time and time again, by the power of His Words.

Jesus made a decision to go to the cross. He could have said "no" but He submitted to God's will, and went. He could have called down legions of angels to save Him. He went to the cross by His own free will. The Word of God makes it clear that the entire way up to his death, Jesus made the choice to die on our behalf and He could have stopped it at any time. It was that humble choice that He made that demonstrated His love towards humanity all the more powerful. The Word says, "Do you think I cannot call on my Father, and he will at once put at my disposal more than twelve legions of angels? But how then would the Scriptures be fulfilled that say it must happen in this way?"(Matthew 26:53-54)

In John 10:18 when Jesus is talking about His life, He says, "No one takes it from me, but I lay it down of my own accord. I have authority to lay it down and authority to take it up again. This command I received from my Father."

Jesus' humility gave Him power. He had to go to the cross in humility but we can't forget He also chose to go with authority. Jesus having the keys of death also means He has the power to release from death those who receive His free gift of salvation. Here is where we all come in.

Jesus fought the enemy with humility, but we cannot forget that He also fought the enemy, and won, with authority. We need to study the authority of Christ because just like we are to emulate Jesus' humility, we are also supposed to walk in the authority that Jesus died for us to have.

The Authority of Christ

Matthew 7:28-29: "When Jesus had finished saying these things, the crowds were amazed at his teaching, because he taught as one who had authority, and not as their teachers of the law.

Matthew 28:18: Then Jesus came to them and said, "All authority in heaven and on earth has been given to me."

All authority, means ALL authority to me. What about Satan's authority? Does he have any? Does he have authority over us? Not according to The Word of God. Colossians 2:13-15: When you were dead in your sins and in the uncircumcision of your flesh, God made you alive with Christ. He forgave us all our sins, having canceled the charge of our legal indebtedness, which stood against us and condemned us; he has taken it away, nailing it to the cross. And having disarmed the powers and authorities, he made a public spectacle of them, triumphing over them by the cross."

Can we please camp here for a while? First let's look at Colossians 2:13: "When you were dead in your sins and in the uncircumcision of your flesh, God made you alive with Christ." He forgave all of our sins. Does all mean some? Does all mean, the not so gruesome ones? Does all mean the ones that most people do? Does all mean all or some? All means All! All means the sins of your past, present, and future. Ok, that is the first bit of good news. Now let's keep reading.

Colossians 2:14 says, "having cancelled the charge of our legal indebtedness, which stood against us and condemned us, he has taken it away, nailing it to the cross." To me, cancelled means finished, over, gone, not happening. Let me tell you, when school was cancelled because of a snow day when we were little, I had no temptation to figure out a way to get there, whether there was a teacher there or not. School canceled meant cancelled. It's the same situation with our sin. Why do we hear that our charge of legal indebtedness to sin is cancelled but then still feel guilty for it? Why do we keep wanting to drag up our old sins and allow the enemy to remind us of them as often as he can and as if we are still guilty?

You need to realize that if there is a snow day and school is cancelled, you aren't going to show up for school, and if your debt to sin is cancelled, you aren't supposed to keep showing up at your imaginary sin debtor meeting with the devil.

The Word says that Jesus took it away, nailing it to the cross. If our sins aren't there anymore but we are still feeling the guilt, shame and debt of them, we have to begin to realize that we are being deceived. Here is the biggie. Get this! Take notes on this! Highlight it! Tweet it! Whatever you need to do to remember it because it is good! Colossians 2:15 teaches us that Satan is disarmed.

"And having disarmed the powers and authorities, he made a public spectacle of them, triumphing over them by the cross." Jesus disarmed Satan at the cross. He took away any ammunition that he had against us. He took away Satan's power. He took away his authority over us. He took it away. It's not there. My friend, if you are fighting Satan daily and feeling defeated, please know that you are fighting an enemy who is shooting with blanks. You are actually letting an unarmed adversary take you down. Yes, I said, Satan is shooting with blanks.

Jesus made a public spectacle of the devil and of Satan's demons when he died and rose from the grave for us. Personally, I think how cool it would have been to see that in the spiritual realm. I would have paid all that I had to see Jesus disarm him. I would have sold all I that own to buy a ticket for that show. Our Jesus beat the enemy with humility and authority. He did it for us. It's done.

Jesus' authority is made available to us. We are able to walk in the same kind of authority that Jesus walks in, because of what Jesus did for us. We have Jesus' authority. The truth is, sometimes we forget that we have it. We simply have to stop being deceived by our unarmed adversary. The devil is a coward and a liar and it's about time that we shut his mouth once and for all about the authority that we have.

Yes, we have authority, right now as born again, baptized believers, we have authority in the name of Jesus to demolish any strongholds of the enemy. We have authority to lay hands on the sick and they shall recover. We have authority to trample on serpents and scorpions. We have the authority to cast out demons and raise the dead. My friend, there is power in the name of Jesus to break any stronghold of the enemy and there is power to walk in the victory that is available to us right now. We have to remember that we have authority and we have to learn how to walk in it.

We have to walk out things with God. I repeat, we have to walk out things with God. God makes us walk in The Spirit and God makes us walk out our spiritual life here on earth. God makes us walk out our authority. God doesn't save us, fill us with His Spirit, anoint us and send us out for us to sit on our spiritual butts and constantly question;

When God when?
Why God why?
Lord please fix this, Lord please help me with this.

Most of our victory that we will experience as believers, has to be walked out. We have to learn how to walk in the authority that we receive when we are filled with the Holy Spirit. I want us to get a holy boldness concerning our authority in Christ. I want us to get a holy forcefulness concerning our authority in Christ.

Maybe you are thinking, *"That's great Mo, but I'm not bold. I'm not forceful at all. I've done the personality tests Mo, I'm not a lion. I'm a golden retriever. I don't know how to be forceful or bold."*

Here's what I'm going to tell you. It's ok, I don't want you to be bold or forceful in your own strength. I want you to learn how to trust in the power of The Holy Spirit that lives on the inside of you, that looks exactly like the Holy Spirit on the inside of all of us, and the Holy Spirit that looks just like Jesus!

Matthew 11:12 reads, "From the days of John The Baptist until now, the Kingdom of Heaven has been forcefully advancing, and forceful men lay hold of it." First of all, let's talk about who is saying this. It's Jesus. He is talking about his cousin who is about 6 months older than Him, John the Baptist.

Jesus is pretty fond of John the Baptist. Just a couple scriptures ahead he says, "I tell you the truth; among those born of women, there has not risen anyone greater than John the Baptist." Jesus is actually saying, there is no one greater.

Not Noah,

Not Abraham

Not Elijah

Not Joshua.

Truthfully, this is a pretty high honor that Jesus is giving to John. Wow! Why John? Well, let's learn a little bit about John the Baptist to see why Jesus says, "among those born of women, there has not risen any greater."

Luke 1:1-17 reads, "Then an angel of the Lord appeared to him (this is

Zechariah, Jesus' Uncle), standing at the right side of the altar of incense. When Zechariah saw him, he was startled and was gripped with fear. But the angel said to him, "Do not be afraid Zechariah; your prayer has been heard. Your wife Elizabeth will bear you a son, and you are to give him the name John. He will be a joy and a delight to you, and many will rejoice because of his birth, for he will be great in the sight of the Lord. He is never to take wine or other fermented drink, and he will be filled with the Holy Spirit even from birth. Many of the people of Israel will he bring back to the Lord their God. And he will go on before the Lord in the spirit and power of Elijah, to turn the hearts of the fathers to their children and the disobedient to the wisdom of the righteous-to make ready a people prepared for The Lord."

There is so much in here that I want to talk about. First of all, Zechariah and Elizabeth are way past child bearing age. They probably had assumed that they were not having kids. The Word says Zechariah says; "But, I'm an old man, and my wife is way past child bearing age."

Guess what? When God says you're going to have a baby; you're going to have a baby. Here's the first lesson you need to learn in order to walk in your authority with God; quit trying to figure out God! He's God and we aren't. The Word says that we have the mind of Christ. The mind of Christ is a mind that walks according to the Word of God. We may have the mind of Christ, but we will not always understand the ways of God. We probably won't understand how God made the sun stand still for Joshua for a whole day, how he parted the red sea for Moses and the Israelites, how he used to donkey to speak and how He fed 5000 with the amount of food in a little boy's lunchbox. No, we aren't going to fully understand God, He is supernatural. But my friend, God will show Himself to you, if you allow Him. Vs. 15 says, "He will be great in the sight of the Lord. He is never to take wine or other fermented drink and he will be filled with The Holy Spirit, even from birth."

Now we are getting somewhere in trying to figure out why Jesus says in Matthew 11:11"Among those born of women, there has not risen anyone greater than John the Baptist. "The angel told Zechariah that

John was going to be filled with The Holy Spirit, even from birth. Friend, do you know anyone that has been filled with Holy Spirit since birth? I don't. There is no other individual mentioned in the scriptures that was born with the Holy Spirit.

Sorry mamas, I know you may think your child may be extraordinary because they scored so high on the school placement test this year, but chances are, he or she is just like the rest of creation, we need to be presented with the gospel and accept it ourselves before we are able to receive Holy Spirit. But, John was different.

Why? Why do you think God allowed John to carry Holy Spirit inside of Him since birth? Well, just like I said earlier, we can try, but we will never totally figure out God, but I myself believe that God knew John needed something, or should I say someone, to help him walk in the authority that would be on His life.

I would venture to guess it wasn't John Son of Zechariah and Elizabeth in the flesh that possessed the kind of authority needed to preach to multitudes a baptism of repentance, and turning from our evil ways back to The Lord. I'm pretty sure that John walked in His God given authority because He had The Holy Spirit leading Him, directing him and empowering him in his calling.

John had to baptize Jesus. It wasn't until after Jesus was baptized in the Jordan River by John that Jesus started his public ministry at the age of 30. You better believe that if you are baptizing Jesus, you are going to need more than a baptismal tank and a church tee-shirt. You will need the only thing that could even compare to Jesus; you would need The Holy Spirit.

Yes, John walked in authority. John the Baptist knew his mission in life. He clearly understood that he had been set apart by God for a purpose. Through God's direction, John the Baptist challenged the people to prepare for the coming of the Messiah by turning away from sin and being baptized. John delivered his message with the force of authority.

How did He do it? Holy Spirit! Jesus said in Matthew that since the time of John the Baptist until now the Kingdom has been advancing. Once again in scripture, Jesus doesn't recognize the works of those Old Testament heroes, He mentions his cousin, as forcefully advancing the Kingdom. I believe this is because John walked with authority. John preached with authority. John baptized with authority. John even called out the King as he challenged Herod to repent of his sins. Later, that would be to his demise, but do you think God knew that? Of course He did. John was a bold, messenger and mouthpiece for God and he had a couple important messages to preach. His first message was, repent and be baptized for the forgiveness of sins.

John walked in authority because he had Holy Spirit and He walked in authority because He knew He had to say what He had to say. He would encourage those that came in droves out to the wilderness to produce fruit in keeping with repentance. After he would baptize people they would ask, "What do we do now?" He would encourage them share with people in need. He would tell the tax collectors to only take what they were required to. He would encourage soldiers to not steal from the people and not accuse people falsely.

He was bold. Why? He had Holy Spirit.

He was confident. Why? Because He had Holy Spirit.

He was a little weird. He didn't look like everyone else, He didn't wear what others wore, he actually wore animal skin and which was what Old Testament prophets wore. He ate weird things, like locusts. He didn't really fit in and He didn't care. He didn't care because He was walking in the authority that was in him. He had Holy Spirit and He let Holy Spirit dictate to him how to live and he obeyed and it gave him boldness and it gave him authority.

John's second message that he preached was, "Behold the lamb of God." John 1:29 reads, "The next day John saw Jesus coming toward him and said, "Look, the Lamb of God, who takes away the sin of the world."

John knew what his two messages were and he preached them boldly, "Repent and be baptized" and "Behold the Lamb of God who takes away the sin of the world." Those were John's two messages and missions and He preached them boldly and with authority because He was empowered by the Holy Spirit to do so.

He told the people to repent and He pointed the people to Jesus. He didn't care what people thought of him. He didn't act like the world. He was ok with being a little different. All of the authority to share his messages came from Holy Spirit. My friend, that's our message to get out too. "Repent and accept Jesus!"

We can be bold and we can preach our message with authority and power as well, because we are filled with The Holy Spirit. John's authority came from Holy Spirit and so does yours and so does mine. Our authority that we need to walk in daily, comes from The Holy Spirit. We have everything that John had. We have The Holy Spirit that empowers us.

We have Holy Spirt that leads us.

We have Holy Spirit that equips us.

We have Holy Spirit that enables us.

I'm speaking to you as a born again believer right now. If you have never accepted Jesus as your Lord and Savior, you don't have what you need yet. None of us were born with The Holy Spirit. We all must ask Him in. He knocks at the door of our hearts, but we have to open the door and welcome Him in.

The truth is, you have no authority if you have no Holy Spirit. When we accept Jesus Christ and we make Him Lord of our lives, when we truly believe that Jesus died on the cross for our sins and that God raised Him from the dead, it's at that point that He sends us His perfect Spirit, that looks identical to Him and then Holy Spirit dwells in us for the rest of our lives.

We can't sin Holy Spirit away. At the point of our new life in Christ, The Holy Spirit will at that point, never leave us and never forsake us. He becomes the boss of our lives and we are now given authority to carry the message of the cross to the nations.

When we have The Holy Spirit living on the inside of us, we have everything that we need to walk in the authority that Jesus walked in. The Word says in 2 Peter 1:3, "His divine power has given us everything we need for a godly life through our knowledge of him who called us by his own glory and goodness." To live a godly life means that we are able to say no to sin. Because of the divine power of the Holy Spirit in our lives, we have the authority to say no to sin. Once you are born again, then you have everything you need.

We have everything that we need to fight the secondary attack of guilt from the enemy. We have everything that we need to fight any attack of the enemy. We have the authority over any stronghold of the devil because of the perfect divine nature that we carry around on the inside of us.

How do we know that we have this authority? It's in the Word! Matthew 28:18 reads, "All authority in heaven and on earth as has been given to me. Therefore go, and make disciples of all nations, baptizing them in the name of the Father and the Son and of the Holy Spirit." We have been given authority by Jesus to go out into the world and to fulfill the great commission, lead souls to Him, baptize them and teach them the gospel. We have the authority to disciple others because of the Name of Jesus.

In John 16:12 Jesus is talking about The Holy Spirit to his disciples. "I have much more to say to you, more than you can now bear. But when He the Spirit of truth comes he will guide you into all truth. He will not speak on his own; he will only speak what he hears, and he will tell you what is to come. He will bring glory to me by taking from what is mine and making it known to you. All that belongs to the Father is mine. That is why I said the Spirit will take from what is mine and make it known to you."

The Spirit will take what is Jesus' and make it known to us. That sounds like authority to me. Jesus handed the authority to his disciples in the book of Matthew and then he teaches them that when The Holy Spirit comes, they will have everything they will ever need to walk in that authority.

In Luke 10:18-20, Jesus explains the authority that we can walk in because of His name. "I saw Satan fall like lightening from Heaven. I have given you authority to trample on snakes and scorpions, and to overcome all the power of the enemy; nothing will harm you. However, do not rejoice that the spirits submit to you, but rejoice that your names are written in heaven."

Luke 9:1 says, "And he called the twelve together and gave them power and authority over all demons and to cure diseases."

Matthew 18:18-20 reads, "Truly, I say to you, whatever you bind on earth shall be bound in heaven, and whatever you loose on earth shall be loosed in heaven. Again I say to you, if two of you agree on earth about anything they ask, it will be done for them by my Father in heaven. For where two or three are gathered in my name, there am I among them."

1 John 4:4 says, "Little children, you are from God and have overcome them, for he who is in you is greater than he who is in the world."

1 John 5:4-5, "For everyone who has been born of God overcomes the world. And this is the victory that has overcome the world—our faith. Who is it that overcomes the world except the one who believes that Jesus is the Son of God?"

Make no mistake about it, if you are a born again, bible believing Christian, you have authority in the Name of Jesus. But, how do we learn to walk in that authority? How do we learn to take that authority and let go of the fear that tries to trip us up at every turn? How do we learn to cast down the strongholds that set themselves up against the Word of God? How do we learn how to take our blood bought authority over sickness, disease, insecurity, guilt and shame? We take authority by doing just what John the Baptist did. Let's study what that is.

John 2:22-30 reads, "After this, Jesus and his disciples went out into the Judean countryside, where he spent some time with them, and baptized. Now John also was baptizing at Aenon near Salim, because there was plenty of water, and people were coming and being baptized. (This was before John was put in prison.) An argument developed between some of John's disciples and a certain Jew over the matter of ceremonial washing. They came to John and said to him, "Rabbi, that man who was with you on the other side of the Jordan—the one you testified about—look, he is baptizing, and everyone is going to him." To this John replied, "A person can receive only what is given them from heaven. You yourselves can testify that I said, 'I am not the Messiah but am sent ahead of him.' The bride belongs to the bridegroom. The friend who attends the bridegroom waits and listens for him, and is full of joy when he hears the bridegroom's voice. That joy is mine, and it is now complete. He must become greater; I must become less."

My friend, we walk in the authority that John the Baptist walked in by remembering that we must become less and Jesus must become greater in our lives. That sounds like humility to me. We become bold and courageous when we are studying our Word every day and He is becoming greater in our lives. We become bold and courageous when we are praying consistently in the Spirit every day and He is becoming greater in our lives. We begin to walk in our authority when we are serving Him in some way and He is becoming greater in our lives.

The Kingdom of God is advancing today like the time of John the Baptist when we are consistently attending services at a bible believing church and He is becoming greater in our lives. The closer we get to Christ, the greater He gets in our lives and the more authority and victory we walk in against this world and the devil's premier and secondary attacks.

When we walk in the binding and the loosing agreement power that is available to us because Jesus gave it to us, we are powerful. We can break yokes of oppression, we can be set free from habits and strongholds and we can walk in the authority that is ours because of the blood of Christ shed for us on the cross.

John the Baptist didn't seek out crowds, they were drawn to him. When we are walking in the authority that God has placed on the inside of us through the Holy Spirit and when we call on that power by using the Name of Jesus, the Holy Spirit will draw people to us to share the good news of Jesus Christ with them. The Holy Spirit is what draws people to repentance. John didn't go seeking crowds, He walked in his authority and The Holy Spirit put people in front of him. God will do the same for us.

All we need is a mustard seed amount of faith and we can walk in the authority Christ has given us. I dare you to take some authority in the Name of Jesus over some situations in your life. Call on the name that is above all names and watch those mountains fall in the name of Jesus. Jesus humbly went to the cross then used His authority to resist the devil. In humility submit to God. Then use your authority and resist the devil.

Our Faith in Action

1 Peter 5:6-10

"Humble yourselves, therefore, under God's mighty hand, that he may lift you up in due time. Cast all your anxiety on him because he cares for you. Be alert and of sober mind. Your enemy the devil prowls around like a roaring lion looking for someone to devour. Resist him, standing firm in the faith, because you know that the family of believers throughout the world is undergoing the same kind of sufferings. And the God of all grace, who called you to his eternal glory in Christ, after you have suffered a little while, will himself restore you and make you strong, firm and steadfast."

You are going to find yourself in that moment. You know what moment I am talking about, the moment that all of the underlining and dog-earing that you have done in this book, must come alive and be put to use. Right now I want to talk about that moment when the rubber meets the road.

When you find yourself in a situation and the enemy is staring you down like a ferocious lion, seeking to devour you with a negative emotion or temptation; here is how we fight with humility and authority. The following six steps, based on 1 Peter 5:6-10, are crucial for you to work on day by day with God.

1. Remind yourself that you are not alone. God is with you. Say out loud to yourself, or privately if you are in public and unable to be vocal, "I am unforsaken. God is here." (Remember the scripture, "Humble yourselves, therefore under God's mighty hand")Think of a scripture to quote to yourself, maybe, "He that dwells in the shelter of the Most High will rest in the shadow of The Almighty."

At this point in the attack of the enemy, the devil will lie to you and say;

"You are all alone. You are going to fall now!" Whatever the attack may be, we have to remember that though we feel alone, we are never alone.

In the middle of the night, we are not alone.

In the middle of the day, we are not alone.

In a closed room with no windows, we are not alone.

In our cubicles or offices at work, we are not alone.

In any situation, we are not alone.

We have to remind ourselves that we are unforsaken. We have The Holy Spirit right there with us. His promise to never leave us, nor forsake us will never be broken. Remember that you are not alone and say, "I am unforsaken, God is here. He that dwells in the shelter of the Most High will rest in the shadow of the Almighty."

2. Remind yourself that God will deliver you. Say out loud or privately if you are in public and unable to be vocal, "He will lift me out of this. This moment will pass." (Remember the scripture, "He may lift you up in due time")

It is not up to us to deliver ourselves. We can't. After we humbly submit to God's authority and realize that we are only safe under His wing, we must trust that He is going to lift us out of this temptation or attack in due time. God is always on time. He is never late. He will allow us to sit in an uncomfortable situation only long enough to discipline us, grow us or teach us. He is loving and gracious and merciful. Trust that He will lift you up in due time.

This part of the technique forces us to stay in the moment. At this point we must look around at our situations and work at staying in the moment. It is vital that while we are waiting for God to lift us up, we keep ourselves from panicking by staying in the moment.

Sometimes I will look at my surroundings and focus my eyes around me as I wait for this to pass. Thankfulness always works. Suppose you are in the vet's office with your dog and the small room that they placed you in is making you uncomfortable and panic is starting to set in. While waiting on God to lift you up out of the fear, practice your trust in God's timing by saying things like:

"Thank you God for my sweet dog."

"Lord, I love being a pet owner. Thank you for the opportunity to take care of this dog."

"Thank you Jesus for a great vet."

"God, thank you for the car I had to drive here and the health I have right now to sit here in the waiting room."

Thankfulness ushers God into your situation quickly.

3. Share your temptation or attack with Jesus. Say out loud or silently if you are in public and unable to be vocal, "I give this thought to you Jesus."

(Remember the scripture, "cast all your anxiety on Him because He cares for you")God is right there and He already knows what you are being tempted with or struggling with in your thinking. Hand it to Him. If you have to keep handing it to Him, do so. Do not carry it. Keep casting your care on Jesus like you are in a game of hot-potato and the longer you hang on to it, the more you will be burned by it.

The faster that we can cast our cares on The Lord, the quicker the enemy will leave. The longer we allow ourselves to dwell on the attack, or the lies from the deceiver, the more real it seems and the harder it is to return to our peaceful state.

It is imperative to cast our cares on Jesus as quickly as possible and as many times as possible until we are ushered into the peace that we are promised by God. In my book "Building Joy", that is written to help children overcome anxiety, I use the analogy of casting a fishing pole. Sometimes we only have to throw out the line once. Sometimes we have to keep throwing it out there until we have a catch. The important thing is that we keep casting. Do not hold on to your negative thought, temptation or emotion too long. The enemy is trying to get you to dwell on it. The shorter the dwell time, the quicker we feel peace.

4. Thank God for the fruit of self-control. Say out loud or silently if you are in public and unable to be vocal, "I thank you God that I have self-control. Thank you for love, peace, patience, kindness, gentleness, faithfulness, goodness and self-control. They are mine because they are fruits of the Spirit." (Remember the scripture, "be alert and of sober mind.")

The devil will try to get you to forget that you have self-control. Self-control is a fruit of the spirit. When we are born again, all of the gifts and fruits of the Spirit are securely placed on the inside of us when we receive Holy Spirit. These fruits and gifts remain dormant unless we realize that we have them and we walk in them. If the devil can get you to forget that you have self-control. He can keep you struggling.

Self-control is a beautiful thing. It is our power to say no to temptation of any kind. A strong recognition of self-control will help you to fight any habit, break any stronghold of the enemy and resist any temptation.

So much of our fight against the enemy with humility and authority is about remembering. We remember who we are in Christ. We remember what God has gifted us with because of Holy Spirit. We remember the promises of God in His Word. Remembering is what keeps us in peace. The devil is a liar and all he can do is lie to us and try to get us to forget our authority. We must remember that we have self-control. Sometimes I will say to myself. "God hasn't given me a spirit of fear, but of power, love and self-control."

We have to remember. Renewing our minds daily in the Word of God, helps us to remember. Thank God for your self-control every day, whether you are in a battle or not. It is a wonderful gift from God. We need to remember that and walk in self-control day by day, hour by hour, minute by minute.

5. If he has not already left, tell Satan he has to leave. Say out loud or silently if you are in public and unable to be vocal, "Get out of here Satan, in Jesus' name."

(Remember the scripture, "Your enemy the devil prowls around like a roaring lion looking for someone to devour. Resist him, standing firm in the faith.") Let me tell you, at this point in your battle against negative emotions or temptation, Satan has probably already fled because of all of your thankfulness to God and you remembering who you are in Christ and your recognition of God's presence. Satan is probably already gone by now and you are resting in your peace that passes all understanding. But sometimes he is pretty persistent. Sometimes he hangs around a little bit longer. Remember, the devil is no gentleman. He is not our friend. He is our enemy and as our enemy, he is trying to set us up to get us out of our blood bought peace, that Jesus paid the ultimate price to give us. He is shooting with blanks, but rest assured, he is still going to shoot.

At this point, it is up to us to just let him know that he has overstayed his welcome. Resisting the devil is our responsibility. Remember that we fight him with humility and authority. Our humility comes from realizing that God is in the room and that Jesus' name and The Holy Spirit is what truly gives us the power. Our authority comes from walking in that power. Now walk in it! Then, after you have done all of this. You just need to stand.

6) Stand firm while your peace is restored. Say out loud or silently if you are in public and can't be vocal. "Thank you God for your deliverance. I trust You." Then stand as God strengthens you. Remember the scripture ("Resist him, standing firm in the faith, because you know that the family of believers throughout the world is undergoing the same kind of sufferings. And the God of all grace, who called you to his eternal glory

in Christ, after you have suffered a little while, will himself restore you and make you strong, firm and steadfast.")

I know that we don't like to think that God uses suffering for our good. But, the Word of God tells us that He does. Does God tempt us? No! Does God make us suffer? No! God does not do anything that isn't good. The Word says that "every good and perfect gift is from above, coming down from the Father." God cannot do evil or tempt us with evil. But, God does allow us to be tempted and does allow us to suffer, so that after a little while, we can be restored and we can become stronger and more mature.

Trials produce perseverance. There is no doubt about it. The more we face trials and temptations head on with humility and authority. The stronger we get. Then, the more we fight the enemy and win with humility and authority, the more we can help others to do so.

Do you think that it has been fun for me learning how to do this? The teacher has been the student for years and years. I know in my heart of hearts that the devil hates me. He does. I know that he has a special bulls-eye on my life because my life is dedicated to loving God, loving people and helping people find Christ and His peace. So, the fight I am teaching you, I promise you, I learned it by experience and I worked through it with blood, sweat and tears.

I think that the best teachers are those who have humbly walked the walk and not just talked the talk. Oh friend, I have walked this. I am still walking it with you. But, the peace of God that passes all understanding, is worth the walk.

Study these steps. Put them on little cards to practice them before you need them. Write them in your journal. Put them on your bathroom mirror. Do whatever you have to do to remember how to fight with humility and authority.

I hate to say it, but the attack will come. It's inevitable. You just have to remember that you have everything that you need to fight and that you are fighting an unarmed enemy.

Fight like our Jesus fought, with humility and authority.

There is Power in The Word

Do you remember your baptism day? What a glorious day that is when a brand new believer decides to make a public statement to the world identifying themselves with Christ, becoming one in Christ's sufferings and also sharing with Him in His resurrection. When we go down under the water and come up, it represents the death, burial and resurrection of Jesus. Our baptism day is such a precious day as God's children.

If you have not made a decision to be baptized, I guess my question is, what's holding you back? We are Christ followers and Christ followers do what Christ does. Jesus was baptized, so we need to be baptized. Jesus was baptized by his cousin John.

In Matthew 3:13-17 we read, "Then Jesus came from Galilee to the Jordan to be baptized by John. But John tried to deter him saying, "I need to be baptized by you, and do you come to me?" Jesus replied, 'Let it be so now; it is proper for us to do this to fulfill all righteousness.' Then John consented.

As soon as Jesus was baptized he went up out of the water. At that moment heaven opened, and he saw the Spirit of God descending like a dove and lighting on him. And a voice from heaven said, "This is my Son, whom I love, with him I am well pleased."

What an amazing day that must have been. John must have been awestruck and amazed to say the least. Everything that John had been prepared for his whole life came to fruition this day when he was given the great honor of baptizing Jesus.

They must have celebrated like crazy, right? I mean, there must have been a reception with wine and goat cheese and all sorts of goodies there after Jesus' baptism, right? Can you imagine? Well, not so much. Immediately after Jesus' baptism, he was led by the Spirit into the desert to be tempted by the devil.

Jesus faced a time of testing immediately after his baptism. Jesus' testing from the enemy, recorded in the gospels of Matthew, Mark and Luke depict exactly what temptations and trials we must face as humans and the perfect strategy we must learn to use in order to overcome and win each time. Let's read and learn from our amazing teacher Jesus Christ.

Matthew 4:1-11 reads, "Then Jesus was led by the Spirit into the wilderness to be tempted by the devil. After fasting forty days and forty nights, he was hungry. The tempter came to him and said, "If you are the Son of God, tell these stones to become bread. Jesus answered, "It is written: 'Man shall not live on bread alone, but on every word that comes from the mouth of God. "Then the devil took him to the holy city and had him stand on the highest point of the temple. "If you are the Son of God," he said, "throw yourself down. For it is written: "He will command his angels concerning you, and they will lift you up in their hands, so that you will not strike your foot against a stone.' Jesus answered him, "It is also written: 'Do not put the Lord your God to the test.'

Again, the devil took him to a very high mountain and showed him all the kingdoms of the world and their splendor. "All this I will give you," he said, "if you will bow down and worship me" Jesus said to him, "Away from me, Satan! For it is written: 'Worship the Lord your God, and serve him only.' Then the devil left him, and angels came and attended him."

Let's talk this out a little. First of all, is Jesus amazing or what? He is so awesome and I am in awe of Him every time I read this lesson. He had chosen to fast forty days. I have to be honest. My stomach is on an internal clock. If I haven't eaten lunch by 1 pm, I can begin to go from hungry to "hangry." You know what "hangry" is right? It's the anger produced from hunger. I am seriously humbled by our King just thinking about the fasting part. He is so awesome.

Jesus had been fasting 40 days when the tempter showed up. Oh, friend, that devil is calculated and coniving. He doesn't tempt us when we feel strong. Jesus wasn't tempted in town with his friends and closest family members around Him where He could feel strong and enabled to fight easily. The devil waits for a moment to pounce when we feel weak. He waited for Jesus to feel hungry and tired and thirsty and weak, and then he started playing his ugly game.

The first thing that the devil does is tempt Jesus in His flesh. He wants to offer Him something that His poor body is craving. He tempts Jesus to make the rocks become bread.

When we are depleted in an area, the enemy knows, and his arrow that he shoots is going to try to hit you right where you already hurt. He knows Jesus is hungry so he tries to tempt him to forgo his fast and just eat something.

Been there? Ever been on a diet? Have you ever decided to give up something that really isn't great for you like sugar or soda because you want to take better care of your body, which is the temple of the Holy

Spirit? What seems to be the thing you crave the most the second you get hungry? Sugar and soda right? Better yet, he will get you to mix them. Go for an ice cream float. If you give him an inch, he will become your ruler. The devil loves to hit us right where it hurts through desires, cravings and physical needs.

He does this through physical and emotional needs as well. Perhaps your husband hasn't told you that you are beautiful in a very long time. He just sort of comes home and sits in his recliner, grabs the remote and asks, "What's for dinner?" Many times when we begin to feel neglected emotionally by our spouses, and then someone at work or at the grocery store gives us a compliment or two, then our flesh begins to crave unhealthy time with that person, because we want that need met and our flesh is just begging for attention. Oh friend, beware of this trap. I promise you there is an enemy behind this set up just waiting to lure you in.

Jesus overcomes the enemy's attack to eat in the middle of His fast, then the devil decides to tempt him to hurt himself or die. He says to him in verse 6: "If you are the Son of God, throw yourself down." He even quotes scripture here to try to tempt Jesus into testing God to see if God would send His angels to save him. Make no mistake about it my friend, the devil knows scripture and you better believe he will use it out of context to tempt us as well.

The devil literally wanted Jesus dead. He wanted him to jump. He wanted him to give it all up. He waited for him to get weak and he came in with a vengeance. My sweet reader, he tries this with us too. I promise you, he is no gentlemen. The devil's goal is to steal, kill and destroy you. He doesn't want you here to testify to the saving power of Jesus Christ, so he is trying to take you out. He wants all of us out! We cannot be ignorant of his schemes. We must also not forget that he has no authority with us.

Jesus overcomes the enemy's attack to literally kill him. So, then Satan goes for the jugular and tries one last attempt to get Jesus to fail. He offers him everything he can lay his eyes on, if only he would bow a knee to him. Oh friend, the devil will try so many times to get us to sell out for his cheap substitutes in life instead of remaining steadfast in our convictions and trusting in the plans, purposes and promises of God.

The devil will try to tempt us with power and prestige and possessions. If he can get us to take our eyes off of the prize, Who is Jesus Christ, for even a split second and onto earthly junk, sometimes we dance with him for a little while. But, then something always happens. The things of this earth, the idols we make for ourselves and the possessions we think will make us happy, always seem to leave us emptier than we even were before. It never fails. When we take our eyes off of our true love Jesus too long, the devil will try to play with us. Remember, Satan is not your friend.

Thank God our Jesus remembered Who He was. Thank God our Jesus remembered He doesn't need Satan's sloppy seconds. Jesus remembered that He created everything. He was with The Father and The Holy Spirit in the beginning of time. He made everything that Satan was trying to tempt him with. He owns the cattle on a thousand hills. His streets at home are made of gold and His gates of pearl. He doesn't need a thing. He's God. No thank you devil. I'm sure Jesus at this point was like, "Ok, now you're just bugging me."

Satan had no authority tempting Jesus. He stole a little of Jesus' time, but make no mistake about it, our God knew just what He was doing to allow this little charade to go on for a few minutes. Jesus fought the enemy and was victorious, not because He even had to fight. He could have just snapped His Holy fingers and the devil would have had to leave. He fought this temptation and it is recorded so that you and I would know how to fight and win. Jesus was tempted in the wilderness, so that The Word could record it for us to take note of how to overcome. I believe Our God had us in mind. He always does.

How did He fight? He fought with the authority of The Word of God. Jesus quoted scripture. What? You mean to tell me, Our Savior, who holds the keys to death and Hades and spoke this world into being, who formed us in our mother's wombs, quoted scripture? Yes!

I know it's hard to believe Jesus put up with the devil that day as long as he did. He didn't have to. He could have called down legions of angels to fight for him. He could have just said, "Leave Satan, in my Name" and Satan would have had to submit to the Name of Jesus and go. He could have snapped his fingers and it could have been over and Jesus could have been enjoying a feast made for a King. But, He didn't. He chose to quote scripture.

You know, our King Jesus, is pretty amazing at doing hard things. He doesn't sell out, or as my husband loves to say, He doesn't "mail it in." I guess that means, Jesus always gives His best. Even talking about the crucifixion, Jesus didn't have to follow through with it. He chose to go, for us. He wanted to do His Father's will. He wanted to save us. He put aside His own feelings and pain and He suffered a sinner's death on our behalf, not because He wanted to. He did it because He chose to.

Jesus chose to use scripture to fight the enemy, because He had our best interest in mind again. Jesus fought the devil with three words; "It is written" and He quoted scripture, so that we would know how to fight.

Do you think you don't have to memorize The Word? Well, maybe not, but then again, you don't have to experience victory either. There is victory over the enemy's attacks, through The Word of God, when our power and authority are released to fight the devil and win. Simply put, The Word must move from our hearts to our tongues.

The three words "It is written" are powerful. When we say out loud to the enemy, or even to our flesh, "It is written" and we quote the scriptures that pertain to the temptation we are facing, something happens in the spiritual realm. Demons shutter and have to leave, our minds are renewed, our flesh is crucified and the peace that passes all understanding shows up.

The Word on our tongue chases away temptation, and ushers in strength. The Word on our tongue makes the devil run away with his tail between his legs and it gives our angels charge to do what they were created for, to serve and protect us. The Word on our tongue breaks satanic strongholds, fights bad habits and helps us to create new healthy habits. The Word on our tongue is just what it is referred to in the Word. It is a double edged Sword, able to fight the most persistent of spiritual predators. Jesus fought with the Word to show us how to fight.

Over the years, I have counseled many people, teaching them to fight anxiety with The Name of Jesus, the Word of God and The Power of the Holy Spirit. These three weapons are unbeatable when used together in fighting temptation from the enemy. But, there is no shortcut. There is no quick fix pill you can take to experience the kind of peace that the bible calls, "passing all understanding". You simply have to mediate and memorize scripture. Then after you have it hidden The Word in your heart, it must be spoken from your mouth for maximum effectiveness.

Speaking the Word out loud is how we fight temptation, sin, and all of the flaming arrows from the evil one. The Word is powerful, effective and able to take down any spiritual adversary you are facing. The Word works, without a doubt.

Hiding the Word in Your Heart

Psalm 119:11:"I have hidden your word in my heart that I might not sin against you."

How do we hide God's Word in our hearts? We do this through, time in the Word, time in the Word, time in the Word. I would love to tell you that I could quote a bible verse and tell you the book and verse immediately off the top of my head. Quite honestly, there are only a few scriptures that I can remember the chapter number and verse. I blame it on my math struggles. You see, I am a writer and definitely not a math teacher. I love words. I love poetry. I love the magnificence of the sounds of phrases grouped together. Math and numbers... not so much. But, I have hidden the Word in my heart, because it is food for my soul. How have I done this? By spending a lot of time in the Word.

I have spent so much time reading the Word, listening to the Word and studying the Word that when the preacher is preaching at church and He starts quoting a scripture out loud, my Spirit finishes it. I can't always tell you where it is in the book, but I know where it is hidden in my heart. It has become a part of me. I need it and I crave it. I can't get enough of God's Word. I'm obsessed with it.

Hiding the Word in our hearts is crucial in our fight against temptation and sin. The enemy will try to catch you with your heart hurt, limping and unable to fight. Remember that he is no gentleman. He strikes at our most difficult times. We can't wait until a temptation comes to get into the Word, the Word has to be implanted in the garden of our hearts ahead of time. It must be hidden, stored and prepared for us to use at any moment.

We must be pro-active. Do you wait until you get sick or have disease of some sort before you begin to eat healthy and take care of your body? Heavens no! We need to treat our bodies with respect as our bodies are the temples of the Holy Spirit. We need to eat healthy food and take vitamins. We need to drink a lot of water and get exercise and rest in order to prevent sickness from coming.

It is the same with spiritual health. The better prepared you are with a healthy intake of the Word of God, prayer and time with Jesus, the better equipped you will be to fight a spiritual attack.

Psalm 119:15-16 reads: "I mediate on your precepts and consider your ways. I delight in your decrees; I will not neglect your word." We need to learn to delight ourselves in the Word. The Word is my delight, but that kind of love for scripture didn't happen overnight. I used to have to discipline myself just to get in the Word before I started my daily chores. I had to make God's Word more of a priority to me, than 10 more minutes of sleep. I had to set my alarm until eventually my body developed a natural alarm clock. At one point I had to make a decision to carve out time with God first thing in the morning, and stick with it. I had to discipline myself, until eventually, my quiet time with God became my favorite part of every single day.

Meditating on God's precepts has to first become a discipline that you set for yourself, but soon, you won't have to encourage yourself to continue, you will shudder at the thought of missing it, because you will crave it so much. Psalm 119:103 says; "How sweet are your words to my taste, sweeter than honey to my mouth!" Oh yes, I love the taste of God's Word on my tongue.

Pretty soon, morning prayers and devotions, will just become part of you. Then, you may crave evening time with God and His Word. The next thing you know, you will be opening your bible at lunch hour. It truly is an amazing way to live. You have the Book of Life, God's love letter to us which is The Sword of the Spirit, available to you at any time of the day.

I have felt God urging me lately to be more like Daniel was in the bible. Daniel met with God morning, noon and night. I have started doing this, and the peace I have been feeling and the effectiveness I have had in ministry lately has been undeniably supernatural. God is faithful and His Word always works.

Hiding God's Word in our hearts is essential for spiritual effectiveness. We can tell the devil to leave us alone all day long, we can beg God to intervene and we can cry out "Why God why?" Or, we can walk in the authority that God has given us through the Name of Jesus and The Word of God and we can demand to live in the peace that is ours, the victory that is ours and the joy that is ours through our blood bought rights as believers in Jesus Christ.

Freedom is ours because of Jesus Christ. We need to take hold of that freedom and walk in it as God's children. The enemy has no authority over a born again believer in Jesus Christ. The devil will turn around and flee with his tail between his legs, the second you begin professing the Word out loud the way that Jesus did. Psalm 119:45 says; "I will walk about in freedom for I have sought out your precepts." Let's all walk about in freedom today. My friend, dig into the Word. It's truly sweeter than honey.

The Washing of the Word

Posted on October 30, 2012 by momydlo

If you have ever had surgery of any sort, you know that it is very important to keep the incision area very clean to prevent any kind of infection. I have been reminded of this lately, after just having some minor surgery done. I am careful about washing my hands well before I clean and bandage the area, and I have been extra careful lately about germs.

As I was looking in the mirror today at my bandage, I was thinking about how the Jewish priests of Jesus' day would have to stand at what was called the laver before they entered the sanctuary. The brass of this basin would reveal their reflection so they could see where they needed to wash before they entered the Holy of Holies, then they would clean themselves carefully to be as pure as they could be entering.

I am so very grateful that Jesus chooses to live inside of us as a sanctuary for His Spirit, no matter how dirty it was when He entered. We were all filthy with sin, yet He cared enough to lay down His life to make us clean enough to enter Heaven someday.

But, daily we still need to bathe. I'm not just talking about a physical bathing for our bodies. I am talking about a Spiritual bathing of our hearts as the Sanctuary of the Holy Spirit. In Ephesians 5: 26 it reads: "to make her holy, cleansing her by the washing with water through the Word and to present her to himself as a radiant church, without stain or wrinkle or any other blemish, but holy and blameless".

Amen, I know my physical body is prone to wrinkles and blemishes, and stains and if I did not care for it daily, it would be covered with such. How much more does God want us to care for the Spirit that was entrusted to us on the day we made Him Lord? We need to daily renew our minds in the Word of God so that when the ugliness of unnecessary guilt comes our way, we can wash it away with truth, when the vileness of fear or anxiety shows up we can be cleansed from it by The Word, or when the smell of temptations and sin start stinking up our life again, we can bathe in the truths of God's testimony.

Yes, I love my daily washing of the Word. Dive in! The water is always perfect

Casting Down Imaginations

With healing, comes growth. With growth, comes peace. The longer I have been walking in the peace that is promised through a personal relationship with Jesus Christ, the more able I am to cast down imaginations.

When I hear a door slam and I'm just getting out of the shower, I cast down the initial thought that someone is breaking into our home and I trust that it is probably just the wind.

When I hear sirens from the highway near our home, I cast down the initial thought that one of my loved ones could be involved in an accident and I trust that God has my loved one's safely in His hands.

When I see I missed a call from the doctor's office in my phone, I cast down the initial fear that something is wrong and I trust that it's an appointment reminder and if needed, God is the Great Physician and He will send forth His Word and heal me.

Many would say that this is not being realistic, and that we are all given a fight or flight mentality that causes us to always run to the negative to protect ourselves. But, God's Word says in 1 Corinthians 13:7: "Love bears all things (regardless of what comes) believes all things (looking for the best in each one) hopes all things (remaining steadfast in difficult times) endures all things (without weakening).

I've learned to ignore my feelings when they do not line up with God's Word. Our feelings are not to be trusted. Our feelings do not get a vote. Only God's Word gets a vote. Now, there is nothing in God's Word that says that we as believers will escape all pain and suffering. Jesus actually says, "In this world you will have trouble, but take heart, I have overcome the world." The reason I am able to stay in peace during situations such as these is, I trust God.

I trust God if good happens. I trust God if bad happens. I trust God when it's sunny. I trust God when it storms. I trust God when we are in plenty. I trust God when we are in want. I trust God, period.

2 Corinthians 10:5 KJV says, "Casting down imaginations, and every high thing that exalteth itself against the knowledge of God, and bringing into captivity every thought to the obedience of Christ." If everything that we have ever learned about imaginations being good things, and that children are encouraged to use their imaginations, why would we want to cast down imaginations? Why would the bible have a problem with our imagination? It doesn't. The bible says to cast down imaginations that exalt themselves against the knowledge of God, or in

other versions, "set themselves up against God".

Our imaginations are from God. God built us with amazing imaginations and creativity. God gave us imaginations to be creative and resourceful. But, just like everything else in life, what God creates for our good, the enemy tries to counterfeit for our demise. The imaginations that we are to cast down are not the Godly imaginations, we are to cast down anything that sets itself up against the knowledge of God. What is the knowledge of God? His Word! God's Word is what we compare all thoughts, feelings, ideas, revelations, up to. If it lines up with God's Word, it is good. If it doesn't line up with the Word. If it is not in plumb line agreement, we are to cast it down!

How do we cast it down? Well, we first have to take captive every thought, which means, every thought that we think, needs to be sifted through the filter of God's Word. If the thought is not God honoring and Biblically accurate, we should take that thought captive, or arrest that thought. This allows us to take authority over every idle thought our brain wants to think. We truly get to decide what we think about. Our thought life does not get to be in control, we do. Our stinking thinking, no longer is able to rule us when we learn how to take captive every thought and make it obedient to Christ.

After we have taken that thought captive, by holding it up to the Word we have hidden in our heart, if it isn't God honoring, we must cast it down like an idol that wants to rule and reign on the throne of our hearts.

There have been days when I am hormonal or tired or hungry and I am not quite thinking all that clearly that I have to literally say; "Take captive every thought, take captive every thought, take captive every thought Mo."

My friend, I promise you, this is empowering. When you realize that you don't have to think every idle, impure thought that your sinful nature or the enemy plants into your mind, you will begin to walk in authority and in peace, like you never have before. It is literally your choice. You simply have to recognize that it is your choice to make and you have to walk out that choice in obedience by taking captive that thought and making it obedient to Christ.

How do we make our thoughts obedient to Christ? Let's talk through some scenarios. Suppose you are thinking:

- *Oh, I'm so annoyed with this exercise program. I hate exercise, I'm skipping it today and eating cookies.* Taking authority in your thinking, you remember what God's Word says about our bodies and that they are the temple of the Holy Spirit and that we should honor God with our bodies. You learn to say, "Whether I feel like it or not. I have discipline and self-control. I choose to stick to my exercise program."

- *"I absolutely love this guy at work. I don't care if he's married. I think God wants him to leave his wife for me.* Taking authority in your thinking you remember what God's Word says about marriage and that the marital bed is to be kept pure and that we must not commit adultery and that sins done to the body are the most damaging. You learn to say, "God has a man for me. I would never attempt to harm a marriage, because what God has joined together, let no man separate. I will wait for my perfect spouse that God has chosen for me."

- Let's say you are thinking: *I have to figure this out. It doesn't make sense. I need facts. I have to control this situation.* Taking authority in your thinking you remember that God's Word says, "Come let us reason together says the Lord." "Cast all of your cares on me, for I care for you." "Fear not, I am with you." You learn to say, I don't have all of the answers, but I choose to walk in peace. I give this to you God and I am not going to take it back. I choose peace. I choose faith.

The first step we must do in all of our thinking is to recognize that God's Word sits as the supreme authority in all of it. If our thinking lines up with the Word, we can keep thinking it, if it contradicts something that we have learned in the Word of God, our safety and blessing and peace lies in casting it down immediately.

This takes practice. Oh my goodness, it took me so long to realize how often Satan was setting me up to get me to focus on the wrong things and keep my mind wrestling with impure thoughts. It wasn't until I had digested a healthy amount of the Word of God that I realized that my soul seems to be at rest when I follow the Word and my soul seems to be a mess when I don't. It's a daily choice. I still have to choose daily to cast down anything that sets itself up against God's Perfect will for my life.

God's Word is His will. His will, is never opposite of His Word. Make no mistake about it. If you are serious about walking in God's Perfect will, read and memorize and meditate on God's Perfect Word.

Spend some time with God in prayer right now. Ask Him to reveal some thoughts to you that you have been thinking, that don't line up with The Word of God. What steps will you take to arrest those thoughts? (Take them captive) and make them obedient to Christ?

Our Imaginations Are Keeping Us from Trusting God

2 Corinthians 10:5 says, "Casting down imaginations, and every high thing that exalteth itself against the knowledge of God, and bringing into captivity every thought to the obedience of Christ." God calls us in this scripture to cast down imaginations that do not line up with God's Word. How do we do that? Why do we do that? Why is this so important?

We cast down imaginations by recognizing immediately that what we are thinking about is not a God honoring thought. Maybe the thought is lust-filled, maybe the thought is fear-filled or maybe it is jealousy-driven. Whatever the negative thought is, we are to take it captive, arrest it, and make it submit to God's leadership. As new creatures in Christ, we are no longer slaves to our sin nature, our sin nature must obey us. Our Holy Spirit on the inside of us gives us the authority to make every thought that we think, submit to the Word of God. It may not feel like you are in authority at the time, but remember, your feelings will sometimes lie to you.

Lust, fear, jealousy, guilt, or other negative thoughts and emotions are contrary to The Word of God and they are in submission to our Spirit so we must choose to rebuke these thoughts immediately and replace them with truth. I've learned to say to myself, "Not today devil." I say this the second I begin to think a thought or imagine a scenario that is not God-honoring. After I say "Not today devil" I call on the Name of Jesus and I begin to call up The Word of God out of my Spirit to fight my poor thinking. As the Word comes forth, my thinking improves, and my imaginations diminish.

Am I always successful? No! Why? Because sometimes I have waited too long to fight. When I am not immediate in my warfare against irrational and unholy imaginations, the enemy begins to gain ground in my heart. When I allow a poor thought to sit in my mind for even a small length of time, it begins to grow legs. Then, one poor thought, grabs another poor thought, and another negative emotion grabs another negative emotion. The next thing I know, I am knee-deep in poor thinking and irrational feelings. Then, here comes the next arrow.

For anyone who struggles with irrational fears, or any sort of chronic anxiety or OCD, (Obsessive, Compulsive, Disorder), you probably know that the longer you allow your mind to think on a negative thought, the more real it seems to you and then the devil throws a fiery dart (accusation) at you like, "What have you done?" You begin to imagine, you actually did the dangerous, ugly, or heinous thing, you had only imagined in your mind. Too long mediating on imaginations that aren't God honoring, steals your trust in yourself and actually steals your trust in God.

You may think, *"Oh, what does this have to do with your trust in God? I trust God, I just don't trust myself."* Friend, as Christ followers, the God of the Universe lives on the inside of us. We carry The Holy Spirit. Well, if we truly believe that The Holy Spirit, The Mighty Counselor, The Advocate, The Helper, lives on the inside of us, then we should trust that He will not ever let us live out the actual temptations that we have thought out. We should be able to rely on and trust in the leadership of The Holy Spirit.

Proverbs 3:5-6 says, "Trust in the Lord with all of your heart and lean not on your own understanding. In all of your ways, acknowledge the Lord and He will direct your path."

Let's break this scripture up and study it out. "Trust in the Lord with all of your heart" makes me think, *all of my heart means all of my heart.* If my heart is deceiving me and telling me that I messed up, when I really haven't messed up, (imagined guilt), it seems I'm losing in the trusting

God battle.

God's Word says in Jude 24 says, "To Him who is able to keep you from falling and to present you before his glorious presence without fault and with great joy." This word says that Jesus is able to keep us from falling. If we truly believe and trust God with our whole heart, we should be able to trust that Jude 24 is true. Then, this would help us to know that what we have imagined, will not come to pass, if we trust in and rely on and live out God's commands.

Studying on we see that Proverbs 3:5 says, "Lean not on your own understanding." Oh friend, this scripture points out the truth that our own understanding is a complete hot-mess, without the leadership of The Holy Spirit. Typically, we over-imagine and analyze things. Then, when we do not rebuke irrational imaginations and poor thoughts, our understanding suffers. We begin to meditate on these negative thoughts. We begin to roll them over in our minds. We willingly rehearse them in our imaginations and then the devil jumps in with an accusation that we've already committed this act. The truth is, because we didn't submit to the leadership of The Holy Spirit and rebuke the poor thinking immediately, our understanding begins to believe the devil's accusation.

This word says, "Lean not on your own understanding." My friend, we cannot always trust our own understanding. We must lean in to the truths in God's Word and lean not on our natural habits and inclinations that we have always relied on.

We must keep our minds steadfast and holy by moving to the next directive in Proverbs 3:6, "In all of your ways, acknowledge Him and he will make your paths straight." We have to acknowledge God in every thought. We have to stop trusting in our own understanding, because our understanding is sometimes affected by how long we have mediated on negative thoughts and lies.

How do we acknowledge God? We acknowledge Him in worship. We acknowledge Him in prayer. We acknowledge Him in repentance for our poor thinking. We acknowledge Him by running to His Word. We acknowledge Him and we crucify our poor thoughts or imaginations.

We have to trust in The Lord, and not our own will. We have to trust in the Lord and not on our own thinking. We have to trust in the Lord and not on our own understanding. We have to acknowledge Him in all of our ways, and when we can do that, our paths will remain straight. Our thinking will stay straight. Our emotions will stay straight. Our actions will stay straight.

If we just follow our imaginations down a rabbit trail, we ignore God's command here to trust Him with our whole heart and lean not on our own understanding. We often try to ask God to help us reason out the very things He didn't want us thinking about in the first place. When The Holy Spirit calls us to rebuke these thoughts and trust in Him, sometimes we have thought about these poor thoughts so long, He has to pull us out of a stinkin-thinkin pit again.

You know what I mean by a thinking pit? We've all dug ourselves a few of these. We've meditated on negative thoughts so long that it's almost like we have dug a hole and buried our peace alive. Then, we cry out, "Why God why? Where are you God? I thought you would never leave me God?" Once again, God reaches His arm down, pulls us out and says to us, "I told you to trust."

My sweet friend, we must immediately rebuke the imaginations that lead us into emotional pits. We can't flirt with any unholy or ungodly thoughts. We must rebuke them immediately, replace them with The Name of Jesus and Scripture, then we simply must trust God. That's our only surefire way to keep from digging our own pit and then allowing the enemy to bury us in guilt.

Imaginations left unchecked are a perfect way to show God that you don't trust Him. Thank God that He gives us a chance to start again.

Repent! Re-start! Re-boot! Trust!

Forceful Faith

Posted on October 22, 2015 by momydlo

Chapter 11 in the book of Matthew really spoke to me today. I felt like God was dealing with me kind of like a high school football coach would his teammates who started to get tired by half-time and needed a little pep talk. It was very early this morning that God woke me and I thought; "Ok Lord, what is it?"

I felt God telling me to persevere. It was like He was encouraging me to keep doing what I'm doing, no matter how tiring and frustrating full-time ministry can get. First He showed me Matthew 11:6 that said; "Blessed is the man who does not fall away on account of me." Well, I meditated on that for a few minutes and I thought. *You know, sometimes when our everyday lives with work and school and raising a family and such can get overwhelming, we have to take in account how we feel about Jesus, and then make Him our focus, and when we do that; we won't fall away. Then, actually, The Word says that with Him as our focus and reason for not giving up, we not only avoid making a mess of our lives, we are blessed as well.*

Wow, I never thought of it like that. It was almost like God was saying to me the same thing He has said many times before, and He has used tons of other scriptures to point out, "Mo, fix your eyes on me to avoid tripping." Yes! That's it! Because we love Him, we are able to persevere!

Then, He took me to Matthew 11:12 that reads; "From the days of John the Baptist until now, The Kingdom of Heaven has been forcefully advancing and forceful men lay hold of it." I meditated on that for a little while as well, and thought;

It takes me being forceful, right Lord? What does that mean? Not ugly, forceful, but forcefully certain that if I don't share the gospel with the lost (because it's not always easy), and other people don't share the gospel with the lost, (because it's not always easy), the lost remain lost. I have to be forceful in my advance, forceful in love.

So, I fix my eyes on Jesus so that I don't grow weary and give up then forge ahead covered with the love of God so I can share that love with the lost. Yes Sir! I'm up for it Lord. Put me in coach!

Wouldn't, Couldn't, Won't

Spiritual warfare isn't a one-time thing. For a Spirit-filled Christian dedicated to doing The Lord's work and living a life pleasing to Him, you better plan on fighting the good fight of faith, daily. Will it be necessary daily? No, we will have good days, bad days, tired days, hormonal days, you name it. We live in a fallen world and we face the same trials and struggles that unsaved people do, we enjoy the same joys and pleasures that unsaved people do. But, on top of all of this, we fight a very real adversary and we have to be on our guard.

I've taught myself a phrase that I speak quietly to myself when a temptation comes on me to sin. I say, "I wouldn't, couldn't, won't." Then immediately I call on the Name of Jesus and I return to peace. It may sound silly that I have to do this, but it is one of the techniques I use that The Holy Spirit has taught me. It helps me to stay in peace of mind and it keeps me from irrational thinking. It is a quick way to take my thoughts captive and make them obedient to Christ. I simply say, "I wouldn't, couldn't, won't.

Breaking it down, I say "I wouldn't", because I would not want to displease God. The Word says in Zephaniah 3:17 that The Lord rejoices over me with singing. I want God to be pleased with me. I know He loves me whether I choose to do right or wrong, but that makes me want to do right even more.

I say "I couldn't" because I would never want to embarrass my family or ruin my reputation and good name. Proverbs 22:1 says, "a good name is better than fine riches." I want to pursue a good name until I take my last breath.

I say "I won't" because I have self-control. One of the fruits of The Spirit is self-control. So, we have it. When we receive The Holy Spirit we receive the fruits of the Spirit. We simply must begin to cultivate these fruits and grow them as we mature in Christ. Because I have self-control, I am able to say no to temptation.

Being able to say, "I wouldn't, couldn't, won't" immediately upon temptation and then speak the Name of Jesus and let it go, allows me to stay in peace. It allows me to develop confidence in who I am in Christ. Knowing and saying what I am able to overcome by the power of The Spirit gives me the strength that I need to fight and win, and be prepared to fight and win next time.

Now, if I wait too long to remember that I wouldn't, couldn't, won't, insecurity creeps in. My over-active mind begins to question whether I am able to fight the temptation. The enemy whispers in my ear that I am going to mess up and that I am not as strong as others. Do you recognize these ugly whispers? I am sure you do, because the devil has no new tricks. He's a liar, a schemer and a deceiver. He is the accuser of the brethren and he will accuse you, even if you have done nothing wrong. If we don't take the thought captive immediately and we entertain it even a little while, he can get you to take his bait to steal your joy.

I have taught this method to my children. My husband Tommy and I have decided that our home will be one of freedom where we speak the truth and combat the lies of the devil. So, in doing this, we have had to be very transparent. We speak about real things with our children. We are authentic and real in front of our children. This allows our family members to say out loud what they are struggling with so that they can get the healing and the peace that they need.

My son Eli is very open and honest about the spiritual warfare that he faces each day. He has shared stories with us about times that he recognizes the devil speaking to him, and how he has noticed it, rebuked it and then called on the Name of Jesus to make the devil flee. Whenever Eli shares, I encourage it. I praise him for his honesty and for his understanding of spiritual things. The last time that Eli shared about an attack of the enemy, I was able to teach him, "I wouldn't, couldn't, won't in Jesus' Name!" It is my heart's desire to see my children and grandchildren and future descendants walking in the victory that I have struggled my whole life to find.

I can't keep anything to myself. I feel as though when God shows me another way to battle, I have to run to my loved ones and teach them, and then race to the keyboard to teach you. We can't be armed enough. The devil is sneaky, calculated and dedicated to our destruction. I have to be dedicated to arming you with whatever God arms me with.

Friend, you may have to call on this method of taking your thoughts captive while you are all alone. You may have to call on this method when you are in the middle of a crowd. You may be having a perfectly nice day, and then boom, Satan decides to try to catch you off your game. The only thing you must remember is that you have authority over Him and when you call on the Name of Jesus, he has to flee. Don't give him a second of your time. When he creeps in, slam a spiritual door in his face by saying, "I wouldn't, couldn't, won't in Jesus Name."

Sometimes you will have to say it once and it will be enough. Sometimes he will shoot another arrow and you have to hold up your shield of faith and say it again and again. But, friend, peace will come. Peace will cover you like a blanket when you learn how to fight the good fight of faith courageously and continuously.

When we choose to say, "I wouldn't, couldn't, won't in Jesus' Name, we please God with our obedience. We also live peacefully with others by protecting our good name, and we grow our trust in the self-control that God has placed on the inside of us, each time that we continue to work out our salvation with fear and trembling.

Yes, "A good name is better than fine perfume." Ecclesiastes 7:1. You smell beautiful my friend.

No Effect

"That offends me!" "I can't believe they did that to me!" "How could she hurt me like that?" "Why would they say that about me?" "That was a low blow! I'm done!" After all I have done for her?" Do any of these statements sound familiar or do they hit a little close to home? I know they do because we live in the same fallen world. We live in a world where we get offended. We live in a world where often the people that are closest to us, offend us the most. Oh friend, get this, eat this, digest this and never forget this; *the one who is trying to offend you isn't the one who did, it's the one who is working in and through the one who did.*

The devil uses offense to gain entrance into our lives. Since he has no way to penetrate the heart of a blood bought Christ follower, he tries to gain access through offense. Let me tell you, he is really good at it. He seems to catch us right where we hurt the most, because he usually chooses to use those closest to us to do his evil work.

Offense isn't as powerful of a weapon if the enemy decides to use a stranger to offend us. He knows that we can usually dust ourselves off and get up again pretty quickly after being offended by someone we barely know, or do not know at all. The devil is not interested in scratching us a little or causing a baby bruise in our feelings and soul. It is the devil's plan and scheme to try to maim us to a paralyzing level. He wants us down for the count spiritually and he knows the best way to do this is to hurt those we love the most or cause us to be hurt by those we love the most.

Remember that the devil is no gentleman. He has no friends. He doesn't have any remorse for any of his attacks. Every time we hurt, he thinks he has won. We have to remember that his time is short. He knows that Jesus is coming back soon so he is working overtime to try to thwart

God's plan of redemption and his arrows are aimed straight at God's most effective soldiers.

Yes, he uses those we love the most to try to offend us. He uses our best friends, he uses our associates and he just loves to use our family to hurt us. I'm not making this up. It's biblical. He did it with Jesus. If he will try it with Jesus, he will try it with us.

In Mark 3:20-30 we read:

"Then Jesus entered a house, and again a crowd gathered, so that he and his disciples were not even able to eat. When his family heard about this, they went to take charge of him, for they said, "He is out of his mind.""

And the teachers of the law who came down from Jerusalem said, "He is possessed by Beelzebub! By the prince of demons he is driving out demons."

So Jesus called them over to him and began to speak to them in parables: "How can Satan drive out Satan? If a kingdom is divided against itself, that kingdom cannot stand. If a house is divided against itself, that house cannot stand. And if Satan opposes himself and is divided, he cannot stand; his end has come. In fact, no one can enter a strong man's house without first tying him up. Then he can plunder the strong man's house. Truly I tell you, people can be forgiven all their sins and every slander they utter, but whoever blasphemes against the Holy Spirit will never be forgiven; they are guilty of an eternal sin." He said this because they were saying, "He has an impure spirit."

Do you notice when the crowds began to follow Jesus because they knew there was something different and special about him, who was the first to buck against it? His family. The Word says in vs. 21, "When his family heard about this, they went to take charge of him, for they said, "He is out of his mind.""

Then, later in this chapter in Mark 3:31 we read, "Then Jesus' mother and brothers arrived." So, I believe it's safe to say that the family that was coming to straighten Jesus out and get him back on track just following the grain and not stepping out to walk in the plans God has for him, was his mother and brothers. Hmm, that one hurts, right?

Satan chose to use Mary and Jesus' brothers to go and stop Jesus from preaching. He had poisoned the thinking of Jesus' family enough for them to say, "He is out of his mind." Then, the teachers of the law and those around him began to say that Jesus was possessed by Beelzebub. Jesus had to defend himself in front of not only the hypocritical Pharisees and teachers, He would soon have to rebuke his own family, who was on their way to "save him" from his mental issues.

How does Jesus respond? Well, first he has to deal with the teachers of the law by letting them know that they are way off. He asks in vs. 23-24, "How can Satan drive out Satan? If a house is divided against itself it cannot stand." He points out their ignorance and He doesn't allow it to penetrate His thinking, His plans or His purpose. He responds to their ignorance with truth and He moves on.

Then, He has to deal with His family. In vs. 31 His mother and brothers arrive. They are standing outside wanting to speak with Him. I am sure Mary is thinking as a mother, *ok, this is enough Jesus. All of this ministry is taking too much of a toll on you, you can't even eat. Now, let's just slow it down a bit."* Mary is still human remember. She carried Jesus in her womb. She had to teach him at 2 years old how to behave. Mary still sees Jesus as her son. Sometimes I'm sure she would forget that He is also The Son of God. Mary had no idea that showing up ready to let Jesus know that things were getting a little out of control, that she was playing right into the enemies plan. But, Jesus knew.

Jesus responded with a little technique that I believe God has shown me in battling the enemy's tactic of offense. Jesus responded with "No effect!" Jesus did not even let them in. Because Jesus is all knowing, I believe He even knew why Mary and his brothers were there. They weren't there to help Him draw more crowds to share His teaching and aid Him in healing and serving. They were there to get Him back in submission to the laws of man. So, Jesus responded with "No effect!"

Mark 3:31-34 New International Version (NIV)

Then Jesus' mother and brothers arrived. Standing outside, they sent someone in to call him. A crowd was sitting around him, and they told him, "Your mother and brothers are outside looking for you."

"Who are my mother and my brothers?" he asked. Then he looked at those seated in a circle around him and said, "Here are my mother and my brothers! Whoever does God's will is my brother and sister and mother."

I have to admit, when I was a new Christian and I read this, this scripture offended me. I was bothered that Jesus so quickly called complete strangers who had become His disciples, His family, and He wasn't recognizing his own family as superior to them. I mean, after all, Mary birthed Him. Mary carried Him in her womb. She raised Him his whole life and made Him a God-honoring man. I remember thinking this. But, not today. As The Holy Spirit has matured me, I have come to realize that Jesus did exactly what He needed to do that day, to remain in God's Perfect will for His life. His family needed to realize that things had changed. Jesus had a mission, it had to be fulfilled and He had to step out from being fully man (who Mary and His brothers knew and loved) and He had to step into His role as fully God (His true identity and Who we all need to know to be saved).

Jesus had to thwart the enemy's plan to let Mary and his brothers in, because He had work to do. He had people to heal. He had demons to cast out. He had dead people to raise. He had you and me to save. If Jesus had opened that door immediately and allowed them in, the enemy could have used them to offend Him.

Yes, the enemy uses those closest to us to try to offend us. He tries to get our family and loved ones worked up about the changes that they see in us. People generally do not like change, even good change. The devil preys on this and he works on the emotions and insecurities of those around us to try to use them to hurt those people who are dedicated to serving Him wholeheartedly. Are the people we love evil? Heavens no! I believe that 99 % of the time they don't even know they are being used in his schemes. They simply become affected in their emotions enough to succumb to his temptation, they take his bait and he uses them to gain ground.

How do we fight it? "No effect!" We learn to not let the devil's offenses affect us. We learn to recognize that he has no authority with us except what we hand over to him, and if we don't allow him to offend us and if we don't allow him to use others to hurt us, we can maintain our position and continue marching.

Remember that we war not against flesh and blood. "For we wrestle not against flesh and blood, but against principalities, against powers, against the rulers of the darkness of this world, against spiritual wickedness in high places." (Ephesians 6:12) Our family members and those we love and even those random people Satan chooses to use, are not our enemies. They are not the ones that we are waging war against. Our war is in the Heavenly realm. It is spiritual. When we can remember that, we can remain unoffended.

When we can learn to say, "No effect" to insults, persecution, judgmental spirits, and jealousy and the insecurities of others, we can remain unoffended and we can stay in position. It is the devil's plan for us to get our feeling hurt so that we will defend ourselves. He wants to try to get us to wage war against the people around us, so that he can get our eyes off of the one we are to be overcoming, who is him.

Remember, that most of the time the people that offend us just think they are responding to natural feelings, likes, dislikes, and opinions. They don't even realize that the devil is pitting them against us to create disunity and to get us unarmed in the actual battle which is against him and his demonic forces. If the devil can gain access in this manner, he can steal our joy, our attention, our plans and ultimately if we let him, our testimony.

Take heart my friend, Jesus overcame the world and you can overcome the devil's trap of offense. Let me teach you a little phrase. "No effect!" Say it right now. "No effect!" You have to be prepared to speak and live and move in "No effect" for the rest of your days here on earth pursuing God's purpose for your life. You will have to recognize when the devil is trying to offend you through others, and you will have to learn how to stand against it, just the way Jesus did.

Did Jesus stop loving his mother and brothers? Heavens no! They marched with Him right up until His last breath here on earth. But, did Jesus allow them to interfere with His work that He was doing that day? No! He responded with "No effect!"

How do we respond with "No effect!"? We don't fight back. We don't retaliate. We don't fight passive aggressive slurs and comments with passive aggressive slurs and comments. We don't pick out the flaws in people, and try to hurl them back at people in order to retaliate. We don't fight back in the natural. We simple say what Jesus says when He is on the cross dying for those who hung Him there. He looked up to Heaven and He says, "Forgive them Father, for they know not what they do."

We forgive. We forget. We move on. We do what Jesus did. That's how we fight offense. We do not let it enter. We must protect the work that God has called us to do. Offense is overcome simply, by not letting it affect us. But, if it does offend us and we get caught off guard, we must immediately recognize it and forgive.

Forgiveness is the antidote to offense. Forgiveness ushers us into peace. Un-forgiveness feeds the enemy. Forgiveness starves him to death. Remember, our fight isn't against people. People are who we are sent to love and point to Jesus. We can't let the enemy trick us into believing that our fight is against man. Our fight is in the spiritual realm. We must wage war spiritually. We do this by learning to say and walk in "No effect!" We do this by forgiving and forgetting.

Many will say, "I can forgive, but I can't forget." I'm going to challenge you to ask God to help you forget, because in forgetting, we are able to maintain ground. You know, Jesus forgets our transgressions. He doesn't just forgive them. He chooses to forget. Micah 7:19 says," You will again have compassion on us; you will tread our sins underfoot and hurl all our iniquities into the depths of the sea." God doesn't just forgive us then write it down to later use against us. He hurls our sins into the sea so that He is able to forget them. If God can do that with our ugly junk and mess and sin, we need to work on doing that for others.

I want you to think right now about someone who may have offended you lately. Take a second and say, "No effect!" Now, pray for them, forgive them, and stand up and regain your position. My friend, every time you do this, you will become stronger and more able to do this until Jesus returns. We must wage war against our true enemy, Satan. Don't get distracted. Don't forget that forgiveness makes us powerful.

Taken Advantage Of

Posted on December 11, 2012 by momydlo

How true it is, that the second we open our eyes in the morning, we have a choice to make. We must choose what to focus our thinking on. Satan will make a bid for your thoughts immediately out of the gate. He will remind you of what you didn't accomplish the day before, what you did the day before that might not have been perfect, and who may have hurt your feelings recently.

I can go to bed clothed in the Spirit, and wake up needing to desperately run to the foot of Jesus to escape my selfishness. There is no doubt that Satan is a master at waiting to pounce, like a "roaring lion seeking who he may devour". It is imperative that we recognize his schemes once and for all to achieve the freedom in Christ that we desire.

This morning I woke up feeling a little taken advantage of in a situation. And, oh how these feelings felt so warranted while I was hiding under my warm covers in bed. I laid there and thought, "Wow, a thank you card would have sufficed." Then, I walked out and began my bible study.

I turned to the book of Hosea. The book of Hosea is such a beautiful depiction of God's unchanging love for Israel, no matter how Israel treats Him. It is so cool to see how God is pretty much ticked off at Israel in one chapter, He is ready to take them down in one swipe and then He calms down in the next chapter and wraps them up in His love again.

While I was praying, I told God that I felt taken advantage of, and do you know what He said to me? "Good, now you know how I feel when you do that to me." How often do we forget the pits that God has pulled us out of? How often do we forget the healings that He granted? How often do we forget the forgiveness that He has given us? How often do we forget, and never write Jesus a thank you note?

Yes, God does want us to feel appreciated, loved, and cherished. But, sometimes He may care more about breaking more of that outermost man in all of us that thrives on selfishness. I love Jesus! I am grateful for all of His provisions and love. I'm sorry Lord. Can this please serve as a thank you note for today?

Be Sober Minded

1 Peter 5:8-9 English Standard Version (ESV**)**

"Be sober-minded; be watchful. Your adversary the devil prowls around like a roaring lion, seeking someone to devour. Resist him, firm in your faith, knowing that the same kinds of suffering are being experienced by your brotherhood throughout the world."

One of my favorite places to minister is at the local prison chapel. When Jesus encouraged the disciples to feed the hungry, help the weak, visit the lonely and imprisoned, I have to admit, I always hoped He didn't mean that I had to. I always wanted to steer clear of ministering in prison as even the thought of it, gave me anxiety. I thank God that a couple years ago, God got a hold of me and encouraged me to push through this fear with faith, because it has been life changing for me since that day.

Now I see those women who I have ministered to as people, not as criminals. I see them as human beings like me who face a true enemy, who is a bully. They simply didn't have the correct ammunition (Jesus and His Word) with which to fight with. So many of the women at the federal prison chapel where I have ministered, are such lovely, Spirit filled women who found Jesus on the floor of a jail cell. Jesus scooped them up, poured out His blood over their sins and gave them His Word to heal them. Pretty much, that is all of our testimony, just in a little different setting.

Some of us were found by Christ sitting on a bar stool. Some of us were found by Christ in the arms of a man that wasn't our husband. Some of us were found by Christ lonely at home with no one to talk to except a couple toddlers we were responsible for. We all have been found by Christ at different times. It's up to us to simply decide, what we will do with this new precious relationship. Will we guard it with all diligence and pursue God with the utmost of obedience, or will we return to our cell floor where He found us, defaulting back to the defense mechanisms and habits we have relied on for so long?

I think I was most surprised the first day I visited the prison to see that most of these women were filled with a peace that can only come from The Holy Spirit and from spending time in God's Word. I guess I thought I would see more of the things I have seen on TV and movies. I spoke with the chaplain and said, "These women are amazing." She explained to me that many of them were incarcerated because they found themselves yoked with someone who was no good for them and many of them were not sober when they did what they did. What a sobering awakening when you have your full sobriety back, and you find yourself incarcerated with your life turned upside down.

The truth is, God's Word warns us about staying sober. The Word actually says, "sober-minded." We must be sober- minded, because quite honestly, we don't fight the enemy effectively if we are not. When we are under the influence of drugs or alcohol, our ability to recognize demonic activity, (Satan's schemes and plans), are dulled and weakened. When God calls us to be sober, it is for our protection.

According to https://www.alcoholrehabguide.org/alcohol/crimes/, "A number of individuals that serve time in jail have committed alcohol-related crimes. Offenses range from minor to serious and include property crime, public-order offenses, driving while intoxicated, assault and homicide. On average, roughly 40 percent of inmates who are incarcerated for violent offenses were under the influence of alcohol during the time of their crime. Many of these criminals had an estimated blood alcohol content (BAC) level of more than three times the legal limit at the time of their arrest.

Finding yourself incarcerated because of partaking in too much alcohol or drugs is not the only risk we step into when we aren't sober-minded. Sexual sin happens because of our inability to fight the good fight of faith in this matter as well.

According to http://abcnews.go.com/Health/story?id=116837&page=1, "Drinking and doing drugs often leads young people to engage in more sexual activity than they intended to partake in, and more importantly, to unprotected sex, says Joseph Califano, former U.S. secretary of health, education and welfare and president of The National Center on Addiction and Substance Abuse at Columbia. Overall, 29 percent of sexually active 15- to 24-year-olds surveyed say that they have "done more" sexually than they had planned while drinking or using drugs, and 74 percent say their peers "often do not use condoms when they are drinking or using drugs."

Let's be honest, drug use of any sort, whether it is alcohol or drugs lowers our inhibitions. It lessons our ability to recognize dangerous situations. It numbs us from thinking about consequences. Quite frankly, it gives the devil an easier target to hit. When we are under the influence we stay longer than we would stay, we say more than we should say and we play things we shouldn't play.

God's Word encourages us to be sober to protect us. God has an amazing plan for our lives, plans to prosper us, and not to harm us, plans to give us hope and a future. Satan's plan is to steal, kill and destroy. When we can stay sober-minded, we are able to pursue God's plan for our life in a more direct, focused and safe way.

When Peter says, "be sober-minded and watchful" the next thing he mentions is your adversary, the devil. We have to be able to be watchful. We have to be able to recognize the devil's tactics. We have to be able to keep ourselves from being ignorant of his schemes. When we are under the influence, our "watcher" is messed up. When we are under the influence and not sober-minded, Satan comes in from behind and catches us off guard.

I have to be honest, I love being in control. I hate feeling out of control in any situation. That is why I do not partake in alcohol and I really try to do natural remedies for any kind of treatment that my body may need.

Of course modern medicine is needed sometimes and God does work through modern medicine as well. But, sometimes all of the side effects listed on drug commercials scare me more than the actual ailment the drug was produced to fight in the first place.

Being in control allows me to be on my guard against the enemy's schemes. 1 Corinthians 16:13-14(NIV) says, "Be on your guard; stand firm in the faith; be courageous; be strong. Do everything in love." Being in control helps me to be a better mother, wife, and woman of faith. Mothers and fathers, I am going to tell you, drunkenness keeps us from pouring into our family the best way possible. Being under the influence of drugs and alcohol keeps people trapped in selfishness, unable to love the way God wants us to love, selflessly and with humility.

The enemy will be able to cause more marital fights, divorces, adultery, and child abuse when drugs and alcohol are continually on the scene. There is no doubt that drugs play a key role in Satan's plans to steal, kill and destroy. So, as believers, we can thwart many of the plans of the enemy simply by staying sober- minded and alert.

Marriages can be saved, children can be protected and lives and futures can be preserved, by obeying 1 Peter 5:8, "be sober minded and watchful." Since most of our spiritual warfare has to do with releasing control back to God, and trusting, isn't this nice that God gives us something we actually have some control over? We have control of ourselves. Be self-controlled. Be alert. Be sober minded. We have a future to protect. Stand on a wall and watch.

Obedience is The Opposite of A Questioning Spirit

In this chapter we are going to talk about Obedience.

Obedience to God.

Obedience to His Word.

Obedience to His Spirit leading us.

Obedience to His promptings of us.

We need to be like obedient sheep that follow The Good Shepherd wherever He leads us. Jesus says in Matthew, when the Son of Man comes in His glory, He will separate the sheep and the goats. Friend, we want to be sheep right?

My husband and I went and watched a documentary on Fred Rogers (Mr. Rogers) called, "Won't you be my neighbor?" He was such a beautiful example of a sheep. He was an ordained minister; I didn't know that before the movie. He loved people. He simply loved God and loved people. When his wife spoke at the end of the documentary, she said something like, "I remember Fred asking me at the end of his life, "Do you think I was a sheep honey?" She said, Fred, if anyone was a sheep it was you."

My friend, we don't want to be goats, do we? Goats are rebellious. Goats do what they want, they eat what they want, they step on what they want. Sheep simply follow The Shepherd. We need to be sheep. When we are obedient to God then we are sheep.

1 John 5:1-4 reads, "Everyone who believes that Jesus is the Christ is born of God, and everyone who loves the father loves his child as well. This is how we know that we love the children of God: by loving God and carrying out his commands. In fact, this is love for God: to keep his commands. And his commands are not burdensome, for everyone born

of God overcomes the world. This is the victory that has overcome the world, even our faith."

Ok, let's dig in here. This says, that everyone who loves the Father loves his child as well. So, first of all, who is John talking about here? Us, He's talking about Jesus and us. We are all the children of God.

We are co-heirs with Christ.

We are brothers and sisters in the faith.

We are daughters and sons of the King

We are God's children. The Word here says that this is how we know that we love the children of God, by loving God and carrying out his commands. That's how we love God, we keep His commands. We love God by keeping His commands. We show God that we love each other by keeping His commands. How are we doing with that?

I know I do pretty good most of the time, but, then I struggle. Can you relate? This is actually how I am with a lot of things in life, like exercise, or eating right or getting my chiropractic adjustments. I do good, I do good, I do good. Then I get lazy, I eat cookies and I take more naps than walks. Am I the only one?

We get like this with God's commands as well. You know, God's commands aren't just The Big 10. We usually do pretty good with the 10 commandments in general. But, the "Do not lie" one, well, around tax time, sometimes we stretch that one when we take our friends out to lunch and call it a business lunch.

We do pretty good with "Do not covet your neighbor's things" until it's hot out and we hear our neighbors swimming in their inground pool and we are out playing in the hose, doing a slip and slide with a blue tarp and some vegetable oil, right? Come on friend, I'm just being real. We do pretty good, then we get a little off track.

Thank God for the grace of God! Thank God that we aren't under the law anymore, but we are under the New Covenant of Grace!

Though we honestly try in our flesh, the truth is, we need the Holy Spirit to be obedient. We need God's Word to put us back in alignment. We need that beautiful little reminding Holy Spirit on the inside of us.

That precious voice that scripture tells us is reminding us which way to go, all of the time, if we will just incline our ears to hear. The Holy Spirit is our guide into obedience and holiness. The Word says, in Isaiah 30:21 "Whether you turn to the right or left your ears will hear a voice behind you saying, "This is the way, walk in it." Praise God. If we can have ears to hear what The Spirit wants to say to us, we can walk in the way that leads us directly into the Perfect will of God.

If we can just listen to the promptings of the Holy Spirit, follow His Word and love people everywhere we go, we will be just fine. Sounds easy, right? Well, not so much. We have a little stumbling block that holds us up sometimes. We have a flesh, that wants what it wants.

Our Spirits are perfect the second we make Jesus Lord. Our Spirits look just like Jesus and just like the Father. Our Spirits are beautiful and Holy and Perfect. It's our souls and our bodies that need some work. It's our souls (our mind, will and emotions) and our bodies that sometimes get in the way of our obedience.

But remember this:

Your Spirit is stronger than your soul!

Your Spirit is stronger than your body!

Remember that as we pursue an obedient life following The Good Shepherd as sheep, not goats.

Our Spirits are stronger than our souls!

Our Spirits are stronger than our bodies!

Obedience brings blessing.

Obedience brings fruit.

Obedience keeps us in God's Will.

We want to be sheep.

We want to follow the Shepherd.

We want to be obedient.

I sat out watching the sun rise one morning as I was thinking about obedience. God said to me. "Any spirit that negates what God tells you to do is a questioning spirit." He showed me that there are special demonic spirits sent out to get us questioning what God has said, in order to negate our obedience. These are questioning spirits. I wrote it down. Then God began to tell me what He meant by a questioning spirit.

Let's say the Holy Spirit tells us to do something and we are to obey immediately. If we hear another voice beginning to reason our way out, we can bet a questioning spirit is involved.

Maybe God says to us, "You need to go spend some quality time with so and so." You then hear immediately after, "What if I don't get to this? I'm really busy, What if this or that happens?"

Recognize a questioning spirit is involved. You must rebuke it immediately in Jesus Name and obey God's prompting.

Maybe God is trying to tell you how much He loves you during your quiet time. He's trying to pour out His Perfect love on you, then immediately you begin to reason, "How can He love me that much after what I have done in the past?" Recognize a questioning spirit involved. Rebuke it in Jesus' name and trust God's heart towards you.

 If God tells you to do something and your next thoughts are, "What if? Why? How? Where?"; recognize a questioning spirit is on the scene. You must rebuke these thoughts immediately in The Name of Jesus, and trust God's voice and obey Him.

Listen, **ALL** demons have to flee at the Name of Jesus, even questioning spirits. You don't ever have to question the will of God. If it lines up with The Word, it's God's will. If God has spoken something to you, that lines up with His Word, trust it to be God's Will.

We have to be on our guard, because a questioning spirit is tricky.

Anxiety is a questioning spirit

Fear is a questioning spirit

Insecurity is a questioning spirit.

Too long throughout my life, a questioning spirit kept me from God's perfect will for me. Not anymore! Say right now: "Not anymore Satan."

I have to tell you, this has happened a few times since I started have writing. God would speak something to me like this. He would show me a principal like "a questioning spirit" that I have never learned anywhere before, yet the next thing I know it is downloaded in my notes. I would write it down, move with it, then God would say, "Ok, now look it up."

That is how I learned what a questioning spirit was. After I wrote all of my notes about a questioning spirit. I just kept writing, then God said "Look it up." So I researched: "questioning spirit" Guess what I found;

Articles about "New Age Enlightenment"

"Transcendent experiences, like talking with the dead"

"Articles about the Buddhist religion."

I found something that said, "The questioning spirit is the starting point for self reflection." Self reflection is a common thread in Buddhist traditions."

My heart began pounding as I realized, "The questioning spirit that God was showing me, was from the anti-Christ!

Oh friend, please don't take it from me, make sure you check The Word. 1 John 4:3 says, "but every spirit that does not acknowledge Jesus is not from God. This is the spirit of the antichrist, which you have heard is coming and even now is already in the world."

Friend, you don't have to be freaked out about this. But, if God cared enough about us knowing this, we need to believe it. We don't ever have to be afraid of any spirits or demonic forces, but we do have to rebuke them immediately in Jesus Name.

We have to rebuke questioning spirits immediately with the Name of Jesus. They are from the antichrist. The Holy Spirit is our guide and God! The questioning spirit is sent to overpower the Holy Spirit's voice. But, greater is He that is in us than that which is in the world.

We must obey God, period! No questioning

A questioning spirit leads us to fear, anxiety and pain.

A questioning spirit can lead us to divorce.

We begin wondering, "Is there someone else for me? Did I marry the wrong person?"

A questioning spirit can lead us to sell out, The questioning spirit tries to lead us to be lukewarm. The questioning spirit says to us:

"Come on, let's not be so radical here. I mean, you don't want people to think your weird or a Jesus freak, blend in a little."

A questioning sprit will say:

"Come on, love is love, who's to say it has to be one man, one woman, to be married?"

A questioning spirit will say:

"Stop being such a prude. Who says you can't get drunk once in a while. I mean, didn't Jesus drink wine?" No one is going to like you if you don't have a few drinks."

A questioning spirit will say:

"How can you not have sex before marriage? Would you drive a car without test driving it first?"

My friend, the questioning spirit is rampant in our society right now. He does not have in mind the things of God, but the things of Satan. A questioning spirit divides churches, causes disunity and causes people to question their leaders and fail to obey them. A questioning spirit is a rebellious spirit. If you recognize yourself wanting to rebel against the rules, you may need to rebuke the questioning spirit that is trying to manipulate the situation.

Men or women who are trying to steal another person's spouse, will whisper sweet questionings in their ear. "Why doesn't he/she pay more attention to you? "You deserve better. If you were mine..." Come on friend, you better learn to recognize the antichrist at work, rebuke that questioning spirit immediately and trust God.

This is important my friend. I put a star by it when God was showing me this, so remember it. **"Give a questioning spirit no opportunity to speak."** Don't let it in! The second we begin to think on the question, or the lies, which is really what is happening, if we ponder it for too long, begin to roll it over in our minds a little and start mediating on it, Satan has an entrance point. We have to rebuke a questioning spirit immediately. Jesus did, and we have to. Jesus actually called Peter, Satan at one point.

In Mark 8:31-33 we read:

"He then began to teach them that the Son of Man must suffer many things and be rejected by the elders, the chief priests and the teachers of the law, and that he must be killed and after three days rise again. He spoke plainly about this, and Peter took him aside and began to rebuke him. But when Jesus turned and looked at his disciples, he rebuked Peter. "Get behind me, Satan!" he said. "You do not have in mind the concerns of God, but merely human concerns."

Friend, A questioning spirit does not have in mind the things of God, but merely human concerns. We must rebuke it immediately just like Jesus did.

The truth is, Jesus had to die. It was part of God's plan of redemption for us. The death, burial and resurrection of Christ had to happen for our salvation. When Peter spoke against it, Jesus knew He had to rebuke Peter immediately. Peter was speaking merely human concerns, not the things of God.

Goats have a questioning spirit. Sheep submit to the Shepherd. The goats and the sheep will be separated. We want to be sheep. So, we have to submit.

When I decided to mediate on obedience that day I literally had no idea what God was going to show me. This isn't 101 stuff right here. These aren't elementary truths.

I think God wants us on a wall!

I think God is ready for His church to start recognizing the deception that we are under so often because we just think that we have to be.

I think God wants His children telling the enemy to crawl back into the hole that he climbed out of because we all have a call on our lives.

I think God wants to use every one of us, but we have listened to those stupid questioning spirits so long that we have started to think it's our own voice.

I think God is sick of His church messed with! We are his bride.

I think He wants us righteous and ready, with our lamps full of oil.

He doesn't just want us just trying to follow the Big 10! He wants us to be His ambassadors. He wants us to be living examples of Christ, right here on earth, living out God's plan for us.

I think God's sick of the lukewarm, and He's ready to start showing us how to fight and how to decipher spirits. What am I talking about deciphering and testing spirits? It's in the Word. 1 John 4:1 says, "Dear friends, do not believe every spirit. But test the spirits to see whether they are from God, because many false prophets have gone out into the world."

How do we test each spirit? It's very simple. Put the Word on it. Does it line up with the Word? If it doesn't line up with the Word, rebuke it in Jesus' Name.

The Word is it! It's our guidebook. It's our compass. It's our map. It's our safety equipment. It's our life. The Word keeps us obedient, if we live according to it. We can't just be hearers of the word, we have to be doers. The Book of James tells us that we are deceiving ourselves if we simply hear the word but we don't put it into practice.

The Word is the lamp to our feet. The Word and The Holy Spirit, keep us in obedience. The Holy Spirit is our guide into all holiness and obedience. The Holy Spirit will never go against the Word and the Word will never go against Holy Spirit. We have to have ears to hear the Spirit. We must have our spiritual ears open. Whoever has ears to hear, we need to hear what the Spirit has to say to us.

A questioning spirit is a spirit of doubt. When you recognize a spirit of doubt coming over you, you need to rebuke it in Jesus' Name. You may have doubt right now, as you are reading this. You may doubt God actually gave me all of this. I'm going to tell you, right now, recognize doubt is a questioning spirit and you must rebuke it in Jesus' Name.

Doubt is overcome by our testimony. We watch God move, our faith grows and then we doubt a little less every day. Doubt is overcome by the blood of the lamb and The Word of our testimony. If you recognize doubt creeping in, tell doubt, "God did it before, He can do it again" Tell doubt, "Not today doubt! I trust God." Be gone spirit of doubt in Jesus Name!

Friend, Doubts and questionings are spirits that have to be rebuked immediately. Don't give them a voice.

If God says jump, jump, don't ask "how high?"!

If God says walk, walk, don't ask him "where to?"!

If God says sit, sit, don't ask "for how long?"!

Obedience precedes blessings. God is our Father. He wants what is best for us. As parents, we want what is best for our kids. That's why when our kids ask us "Why?", what do we tell them? "BECAUSE I SAID SO!" God doesn't have to explain Himself. God doesn't have to give us details. God's the boss!

Make no mistake about this, God will never lead us where His Spirit won't protect us and His Word won't guide us. The Word is a lamp to our feet and a light to our path. The Word is our scale by which to measure all of our inklings, feelings, promptings, Does it line up with the Word? If yes, keep going with it. If not, rebuke it and obey God.

Disobedience, delivers drama. I have a funny saying that came to me one time on stage. "If Disobedience was a mama, her baby would be Drama." When I'm dealing with someone in the ministry who seems to just be caught in drama, drama, drama, and it oozes out everywhere, I can usually sense a disobedient person.

Disobedient people struggle with authority.

Disobedient people struggle with submission. Disobedient people struggle with conforming to the rules of God and man. They make excuses for their actions and love to blame others. Dramatic, disobedient people are draining. Let's not be disobedient children, and cause drama. Let's be sheep, not goats.

Obedience brings blessing.

Obedience brings peace.

Obedience brings fruit.

Obedience moves the hand of God.

Our Daddy, Father God wants what is best for us. We simply have to learn to say, "Yes Lord!"

He is able

To him who is able to keep you from stumbling and to present you before his glorious presence without fault and with great joy- to the only God our Savior be glory, majesty, power and authority, through Jesus Christ our Lord, before all ages, now and forevermore! Amen.
Jude 1:24-25

You don't have to second guess yourself and wonder if you can actually finish this race. Oh friend, there's no question whether you will be victorious or not if you can keep one thing in mind; you must remember that you are never alone. You must remember that you are never flying solo. You must remember that you are Unforsaken. God is never going to leave you and He is never going to forsake you. Once you have made Jesus Lord, you can guarantee that you have everything that you will ever need to live a Holy Life. Once you have The Holy Spirit on this inside of you, you are powerful and unable to be defeated.

How do I know this? The bible tells us so. You see, there is a perpetual fear that Satan always tries to throw at me, but his efforts fail because I know the truth. Satan will constantly try to get me to fear messing up to the point that I would disappoint everyone around me including myself and God. Satan loves to whisper in my ear that I am one step away from my next pit. I thank God that I found a beautiful truth in God's Word that has been an anchor for me when Satan stirs the waters of my soul once again. The Word says in Jude 1:24-25 "To Him who is able to keep you from stumbling and to present you before His glorious presence without fault and with great joy.-to the only God our Savior be glory, majesty, power and authority, through Jesus Christ our Lord, before all ages, now and forevermore! Amen.

Yes! This glorious word says to me that the God inside me is able to keep me. He is able to sustain me. He is able to light my path, guide my feet, give me wisdom and hold me up. This word speaks protection to me. This word speaks peace to me. This word helps me to be brave. All honor and praise is given To Jesus, who is able to keep me from falling. Jesus is the reason that we won't fall. Jesus is the reason that we remain safe.

The Holy Spirit's power on the inside of us gives us strength. We won't have that epic failure we fear when we are able to trust and rely on and obey that perfect supernatural power that is on the inside of us. Romans 8:11 says, "The Spirit of God, who raised Jesus from the dead, lives in you. And just as God raised Christ Jesus from the dead, he will give life to your mortal bodies by this same Spirit living within you." This scripture teaches that we have resurrection power living on the inside of us. I don't know a devil in hell that can come against resurrection power.

We have resurrection power on the inside of us. We are able to speak things into existence simply because we speak with the mighty Name of Jesus. We are able to fight demons and they have to flee, because we speak the Name of Jesus. We are able to tell mountains to move and they have to move because we carry The Holy Spirit on the inside of us and we know the authority that we have in the Name of Jesus. Our power comes from within. We simply have to remember that with Christ in us, we are powerful. We are weak on our own; but with Christ we are powerful and we are able to fight from a place of victory.

I was driving across town in my old truck to pick up my husband. We have a little trick that we have to do sometimes with our clutch if it starts shifting hard. It was getting dark out and the stick shift started acting up. So, I pumped the clutch a few times at stop lights, because that usually works until I can get brake fluid in. Well, this time, the pumping wasn't working. I found myself driving down the road struggling to shift into the next gear. Fear crept in. I was approaching a pretty busy intersection and instead of panicking, I pumped that clutch and I said out loud, "Ok Lord, I need You!" I pumped the clutch again, and the truck started shifting gently again. Once again God reminded me that I'm never alone. Once again The Holy Spirit took control of the situation and I was held safely in His arms. I pulled into the house where I was picking up my husband Tommy and I told him, "You need to add fluid." He popped the hood and filled it up. I climbed into the passenger seat and looked out the window at the stars and prayed quietly, "You never leave me or forsake me God. You never let me down. Thank you Jesus."

Oh friend, He is able to keep us from falling. He is able to keep us safe. He is able to keep us protected from the schemes of the enemy. He is able. We simply have to remember that He is there. So many times we get caught up in day to day life and forget that The God of the Universe actually chooses to make our daily life part of His daily life. We push through and try to control situations when all the while, God is sitting back, just hoping we will call on Him. He is able to pull us out of pits, rescue us from lions, destroy the flaming arrows headed our way, and so much more. However, it is up to us to remember that He is able, and that He is pursuing that sort of protective relationship with us.

Psalm 121

A song of ascents.

"I lift up my eyes to the mountains—
where does my help come from? My help comes from the LORD,
the Maker of heaven and earth.

He will not let your foot slip—
he who watches over you will not slumber;
indeed, he who watches over Israel
will neither slumber nor sleep.

The LORD watches over you—
the LORD is your shade at your right hand;
the sun will not harm you by day,
nor the moon by night.

The LORD will keep you from all harm—
he will watch over your life;
the LORD will watch over your coming and going
both now and forevermore."

This is my favorite psalm. It screams protection, deliverance, and safety to me. We are able to see where our help comes from. Our help doesn't come from natural defense mechanisms. Vs.2 says, "My help comes from The Lord." This is so true. Nothing here on earth gives me the peace that my relationship with Jesus Christ gives me. Nothing makes me feel more secure than knowing what vs. 3 says, "He will not let your foot slip." Oh friend, nothing makes me feel safer than knowing what vs. 5 says, "The Lord watches over you."

This psalm keeps my nerves from getting out of control. This psalm gives me confidence. This psalm makes me brave. Could you use a little help with courage and bravery? I know most of us could. I thank God for the promise in vs. 7 that, "the Lord will keep you from all harm." Does this say, some harm? No! It says *all* harm. The Lord is our Protector, our Deliverer, Our Sustainer and Our Peace. We simply can't forget that He is able.

Our God is able to deliver us from The Evil One. Yes, Satan has a plan for our lives, but we simply cannot forget that our God is bigger. Our God is stronger. Our God is in control. Satan has no power, except what we allow ourselves to believe that he has. We must stop fearing him and we must learn to stand up to him.

Remember, Satan is shooting with blanks. We have to understand that Jesus already defeated him at the cross and because we are the righteousness of God in Christ Jesus, co-heirs with Christ and sons and daughters of the King, we also have authority over Satan. The Word says in Colossian 2:14-15, "having canceled the charge of our legal indebtedness, which stood against us and condemned us; he has taken it away, nailing it to the cross. And having disarmed the powers and authorities, he made a public spectacle of them, triumphing over them by the cross." This word tells us that Jesus made a public spectacle of Satan and his demons when he beat them at the cross. This also says that Satan and Hell have been disarmed. Hell has no ammunition. There's no winning without ammunition.

Oh friend, you are able to conquer an unarmed, already defeated adversary. You simply must remember that you have authority, because you are a child of God. You have authority because Jesus lives in you. You can fight and win from a place of victory, because Holy Spirit, can't lose.

We must continue to renew our minds in the Word of God in order to grow in our confidence in Christ. Insecure Christians remain defeated

Christians. We must learn to trust in the Lord with all of our heart and lean not on our own understanding in order to stay in the victory we desire to live in. Renewing our minds and crucifying our flesh is a daily regimen we all must learn to live in as we walk out our victorious life in Christ.

To Him, Who Overcomes

I tell people all of the time, "I am an overcomer, not an overcamer." Even though Jesus has overcome the cross and sin and even though He has made a way for us to walk in victory, we still have to be the ones who walk it out. We have to do the walking. We walk out our healing. We walk out our victory. We walk out everything, daily with The Lord. We are overcomers, in Him who overcame.

We all want a wham, bam, thank you mam kind of victory. We want quick healing. We want a quick deliverance. We want a drive-through miracle. Well, I'm sorry if I am the first one to tell you the truth, but here it is, life is hard and we must overcome through Christ. There is a reason why the bible ends with Revelation, because I believe God wants us to remember the points made in this book, and one of the main points made, is "to him who overcomes."

Oh friend, we are overcomers in Christ, but we have to have something to overcome in order to be an overcomer. We will overcome the enemy, we overcome sin, we overcome spiritual battles and we win, every day until we take our last breaths and are with God in Glory. The truth is, we are all either going into a trial, going through a trial, or coming out of a trial. It literally feels like a spiritual roller coaster sometimes. We have dips and turns and times we are just slowly trudging up-hill. Then sometimes life sends us face first down a mountain. But, we are overcomers in Christ. We are victorious in Christ. With Christ we can maintain our peace and composure no matter what part of the rollercoaster we are on.

Do we wish the second we were born all of our decisions were already made, all of our choices were guaranteed to be correct and all of our plans would succeed? Of course we do, but the reality is, free will is a gift from God that we must not take lightly and we must respect the living daylights out of that gift. Every day that we are here on Earth we are given a choice. That choice is to surrender to Christ, or to do life on our own. We must daily make the correct decision to follow His will and His ways if we want to stay in the race, covered in His grace.

Why can't life be easier? Why would a good God allow all of these trials to happen in life? Why God why? When God when? The answer to all of these questions is simple. We live in a fallen world. We follow a perfect God. Someday, if we have made Jesus Lord, we will be with The Father forever in Paradise. Until then, if we can keep our eyes penetrated on Jesus and His will, His Word and His ways, we can live a life full of joy and have so much to look forward to in Glory.

The Book of Revelation speaks of the rewards we will receive in simply overcoming.

"To the one who is victorious, I will give some of the hidden manna. I will also give that person a white stone with a new name written on it, known only to the one who receives it." Revelation 2:1

"To the one who is victorious and does my will to the end, I will give authority over the nations— that one 'will rule them with an iron scepter and will dash them to pieces like pottery'—just as I have received authority from my Father. I will also give that one the morning star." Revelation 2:26-28

"The one who is victorious will, like them, be dressed in white. I will never blot out the name of that person from the book of life, but will acknowledge that name before my Father and his angels". Revelation 3:5

"The one who is victorious I will make a pillar in the temple of my God. Never again will they leave it. I will write on them the name of my God and the name of the city of my God, the new Jerusalem, which is coming down out of heaven from my God; and I will also write on them my new name." Revelation 3:12

"To the one who is victorious, I will give the right to sit with me on my throne, just as I was victorious and sat down with my Father on his throne." Revelation 3:21

The Word is packed full of promises to those who are able to overcome and remain victorious in Christ. I don't see very much in scripture about life being simple and easy with nothing to overcome. Actually, Jesus says quite the opposite. He says, "In this world you will have trouble, but take heart, I have overcome the world." John 16:33. That's it! We are able to overcome, because Jesus has already overcame. He is our lifeline that we hold onto and never let go, which will guarantee our victory. The blood Jesus shed for us at Calvary is what is to be appropriated over every area of our lives in order to walk victorious and free.

We must plead the blood of Jesus over our marriages. We must plead the blood of Jesus over our children. We must plead the blood of Jesus over our families, our homes, our friends, our workplaces, our schools. You name it. The blood of Jesus is what helps us to overcome.

The Devil has no power over the blood. The blood is what saved us all. Satan was defeated once and for all by the blood; and by that blood we are overcomers. Revelation 12:11 says, "They triumphed over him by the blood of the Lamb and by the word of their testimony; they did not love their lives so much as to shrink from death. "We must learn to appropriate the blood of Jesus to our lives and walk in our victory as we do so. We are overcomers in Him. We simply must remember that Jesus' blood is why He overcame for us and so we are able to overcome through Him.

To Him who overcomes there is so much to look forward to. We have so much promised to us, in remaining victorious in Christ. The goal of this entire book has been to equip you with strategies to overcome the enemy and be victorious in spiritual warfare, but it truly comes down to two things that we must do every day in order to stay on our A-game. We must realize that we are three part beings. We have a Spirit (who is The Holy Spirit) living on the inside of us. We have a soul (our mind, will and emotions) and we have a body (this is obviously what we walk around in everyday while we are here on Earth) this is our flesh.

In order to overcome every tactic of the enemy we must daily renew our minds in the Word of God and we must crucify our flesh daily. Every day that we walk around in our earthly bodies we should start to look more like Jesus and less like Satan and the world. We should begin to resemble the things of Heaven and resemble less the things of Earth. We do this daily by crucifying our flesh (dying to self) and renewing our minds (reading, mediating, memorizing and saturating ourselves in God's Word). We renew our minds to think the way the bible thinks, which is how God thinks. We crucify our flesh to make our flesh submit to our Spirit.

God spoke something to me the other day and it was powerful. I was taking a walk and thinking about self-discipline. I was talking to God about how hard it is sometimes to stay on a work-out regimen. I do great, then I get busy and I slack off, then I do great, then I slack off. I asked God to help me with my self-discipline and He said, "Your Spirit is stronger than your soul. Your Spirit is stronger than your body." That's it! That's how we stay in the race as an overcomer, we give our Spirit total control over our soul (our mind, will and emotions) and over our flesh (our body). When the Spirit makes all of our decisions we are guaranteed victory.

In Matthew 26:41 Jesus says to His disciples, "Watch and pray so that you will not fall into temptation. The spirit is willing, but the flesh is weak." In this passage, Jesus had just asked His disciples to stay awake with Him and keep watch. He turned around only to find them asleep. You see, the disciples were following what their flesh wanted and not what Jesus had asked them to do. So, Jesus uses this teachable moment to share with them how to overcome temptation, "watch and pray," and I might add, trust your strong Spirit, it is much stronger than your flesh.

Our Spirit is stronger than our soul. Our Spirit is stronger than our body. We can be victorious over temptation. We simply must "watch and pray" and crucify our flesh and renew our minds, daily.

My Dog Needs A Time-Out Again!

Posted on January 16, 2014 by momydlo

You know that feeling when you are watching yourself, or your kids or someone you know starting to develop a bad habit, and you know you better stay on top of it before it becomes a problem? Oh, my dog Tyco is right there lately. I woke up this morning and found her on the couch again, and let me tell you, she knows….she isn't allowed on the couch. And, listen, before you say; "come on Mo, she's part of the family." : believe me; my dog is blessed. She has way…..too much reign of the house. She is allowed on certain beds, the leather couch in Trav's room, she gets table scraps, she makes every Sunday trip to Grandma's, she is very blessed. But, as far as my cloth couch, my white bed spread, and my daughter's new bedspread, she knows she isn't supposed to be on them.

But, she pushes it sometimes. I truly think she knows more English words than some American's. She knows the boundaries to our yard, and when she is ready to push it; she turns around to look at who is watching, then when I say; "stay in the yard." She turns around nonchalantly like; "Oh, I didn't see you." WAY TOO SMART!

Lately, she has been trying the boundaries. She has been jumping on people out of excitement when they come to visit which she hasn't done in a while, going where she isn't supposed to go and pushing the limits, almost like she is just begging for my discipline. And, so yes, she is getting it. She has spent two times already in her time-out (the laundry room) today, and it is barely noon. But, I know she needs it, she craves it and she will be better off for it. I truly want her feeling safe in her boundaries and rules and only through me being consistent with her will she feel it.

And, isn't that just how we are with God? When we are actively in His Word, studying, praying, and applying His truths to our lives, we are able to practice such better self-control of our flesh. We don't complain as much. We stay pretty controlled with our gossip and we even think the best of others. But, when we get out there on our own and we push the boundaries that God has set for us and we peak over our back to see if anyone is watching, usually we find ourselves in a pinch, needing some discipline.

Yes, we have everything we need in our Spirit to say "No" to what we are supposed to say "No" to and "Yes" to those yes things. But, without the Word planted deeply in our hearts, we often misunderstand the leading of The Holy Spirit where our self-control is concerned. It is only by the discipline of God in our lives and our self-discipline in crucifying our flesh will we truly be able to live a life worthy of the calling we have received.

Discipline truly is a gift from God and we need to be pursuing it daily; whether we are women, men or Border Collies. I love Titus 1:8: "but hospitable, a lover of good, self-controlled, upright, holy, and disciplined."

Pray for me! It's going to be a long day; she just hurdled the ottoman!

Now Walk It Out

I went for a walk and asked God to help me wrap up this book. I told God that I don't know when I am ever going to feel done with this book, as He keeps showing me lesson by lesson how to walk this thing called spiritual warfare out. Then God said, "Then walk it out." I started to jog from the adrenaline of realizing, *that's it! That's my last chapter.* Oh friend, so much of spiritual warfare is just deciding to walk it out.

Dear reader, student and friend, I could keep feeding you techniques, biblical truths and encouragement; but the truth is, until you put these things into practice, it's just head knowledge, and it isn't helping anyone. So, right now, it's my job to send you out. I have to commission you to take your blood bought authority as a child of God and go! Go and walk this thing out.

We know who were are in Christ. We know Whose we are. We belong to God. We no longer are slaves to sin. We are slaves to righteousness. But until we ditch our old slave clothes and stand firm in our robes of righteousness, we will still act like slaves and allow the devil to push us around.

We are crucified with Christ. We no longer live, but Christ lives in us. We carry the precious Holy Spirit. The Holy Spirit is our Helper, our Guide, our Teacher, our Protector, our Deliverer and our Counselor. I could keep going. Because we are the temples of The Holy Spirit, we have everything that we need to live in true holiness and peace, no matter how many arrows are shot in our direction.

We have The Word of God. The Word of God is our sword. We are able to march forward fearlessly because we are covered with our spiritual armor of God and we have our sword up ready to fight and win. The Word of God in our hearts and minds and on our tongues, makes us powerful. The Word heals us, delivers us, protects us and gives us strength, courage and victory. Need I say more?

We must continue to speak the Word out loud to fight our flesh, the world and the devil. The three words, "It is written", are powerful and effective. They worked for Jesus and they will work for us. We simply must hide so much of the Word in our hearts that it flows off of our tongues whenever it is needed. Hide it in your heart my friend. It will save you from every attack.

Renewing our minds in the Word of God and crucifying our flesh daily are what we are called to do and must know how to do until we take our last breath. Tell your old ugly flesh that likes to try to resurrect sometimes that you are dead to sin, and you don't live in it any more. Tell your old sinful nature, "You're dead to me." Reckon yourself dead to sin and feel free to steal this old country girl's phrase, "I reckon I'm dead to this."

Speak life in every situation. Proverbs 18:21 says, "Death and life are in the power of the tongue." What we say matters.

- Stop saying, "I'm never going to get over this habit." Start saying, "I am free indeed and I am a slave to righteousness. God has broken every chain Satan once had on me."
- Stop saying, "I am guilty. I don't think God can truly forgive me for this." Start saying, "I am forgiven, I am justified, God has forgotten my sins so I will forget them. I am free in Jesus' Name."
- Stop saying, "I'm terrible at this." Start saying. "Every day I am better and better at this."
- Stop saying, "This is killing me." Start saying, "I am well. I am happy. I am whole. Today is a great day."

- Stop saying, "The devil is always on my back." Start saying, "I have authority to trample on serpents and scorpion and to overcome every tactic of the enemy."
- Stop saying, "I feel so alone." Start saying, "I know I am never alone. I am Unforsaken. God is never going to leave me, never going to forsake me."

Our Words contain power. What we say matters. Words are things and we have authority over all things as Christ followers. That means that we have authority over our words. Speak life. The Words we say determine what our lives will become. Don't believe me? Give it a try. Test it out. Just see if when you make a valiant effort to change how you speak, if your life takes a radical turn for the better. It will my friend. Words matter.

In humility and authority we fight the devil and win, just as Jesus did. Humility and authority are powerful when combined with faith and directed straight at the devil and his demons. He has no power over you. The only power the enemy has in your life is what you hand to him on a silver platter. Stop letting him trick you into believing he has any power. Remember, he is fighting with blanks. He's disarmed.

There is power in the blood of Jesus to break satanic strongholds of any sort. The blood of Jesus must be appropriated over every area of our lives. Plead the blood of Jesus over your family. Plead the blood of Jesus over your health. Plead the blood of Jesus over your workplace, your home, your cars, and every area of your life. The blood of Jesus is powerful and effective. The blood is what rescued us from sin. The blood will protect us when we can remember to apply it to our lives.

Remember who you are and Whose you are. You belong to God. God takes full responsibility for His children. Just like we as earthly parents would do anything that we could to protect our children from harm, our Father God is ready and able to protect us from any spiritual harm the enemy may try to threaten us with. You are a child of God. Take your seat at the table.

Oh friend, pray. Pray like you actually believe our Daddy in Heaven wants to talk to you. Pray like you believe the words in the bible are all 100% truth and written for us. Pray like you know God never sleeps. Pray like you believe you will be healed. Pray like a warrior who is wearing his full armor. Pray like a son or daughter of The King would pray, with expectancy and faith. Pray when things are good. Pray when things are bad. Pray when your life is quiet. Pray when your life is chaotic. Oh reader, student, friend, pray without ceasing.

Now walk it out. Walk this spiritual walk out. Trust in the Lord with all of your heart, lean not on your own understanding and walk this thing out knowing that God is going to direct your path. Take each step with your feet fitted with the readiness that comes from the gospel of peace. Walk it out with your loins girded in truth. Walk out spiritual warfare with the consistent reminder playing in your mind that you are more than a conqueror in Christ Jesus. Remember that God's grace is sufficient for you, His power is made perfect in weakness, so don't worry if you feel weak. When we are weak, He is strong. Trust that grace is on the way.

Walk it out facing forward. No looking back. Just like Lot's wife turned into a pillar of salt in Genesis 19 for looking back. God is serious about us fixing our eyes forward. The Word reminds us over and over to forget what is behind and press on towards what is ahead. Whether you are tempted to look back at mistakes you made 2 minutes ago or 2 decades ago, listen my friend, don't give in, don't look back. Your victory is ahead, not behind. Fix your eyes ahead, and position yourself to keep walking forward.

You have already won. Jesus already fought the good fight and defeated death and sin once and for all over 2000 years ago on the cross. We are victorious only and always because of what Jesus did at Calvary. You are already seated in Heavenly places with Him. You already have a seat at God's table. The fight has already been won. The tomb is empty. The resurrection happened. Now, you simply have to remember that you have resurrection power on the inside of you. You are able to fight and win any battle, because you carry Holy Spirit. The same power that raised Jesus from the grave, lives in you. We have already won the battle.

So much of our victory is simply, remembering.

Remembering Jesus.

Remembering you belong to Him.

Remembering you are free.

Remembering that your chains are gone.

Remembering you have authority.

Remembering you are loved.

Remembering you are equipped.

Remembering you are never alone.

Remembering you are Unforsaken.

You got this. Now, walk it out.

The Next Arrow

About The Author

Mo Mydlo is a wife of 25 years to Tommy Mydlo, a mother of four, an author, a television personality and a bible teacher. Mo has teaching segments that appear on The Good Life TV45, called "Moments with Mo."

Mo enjoys working full time in the ministry. She is the Executive Director for Unforsaken Women Corporation, a not for profit organization whose mission is to help women renew their minds in the Word of God and to help women and children locally and globally through their mission efforts.

Mo enjoys serving alongside the other volunteers at Unforsaken Treasures Resale Shop, a resale shop in Oakland Florida which supports the ministry and missions of Unforsaken Women Corporation.

Mo loves to cook, volunteer at church, repurpose old furniture and decorate and care for her home. She enjoys spending time with family and friends and she especially loves spending special time with her best friend Jesus Christ.

For more information on Mo's writing and teaching, visit her website at www.unforsakenwomen.com

Made in the USA
Middletown, DE
17 March 2022